IMPROVING TEACHING THROUGH EXPERIMENTATION
a laboratory approach

IMPROVING TEACHING THROUGH EXPERIMENTATION

a laboratory approach

EDMUND T. EMMER

Department of Educational Psychology
The University of Texas at Austin

GREGG B. MILLETT

Department of Curriculum and Instruction
The University of Texas at Austin

Prentice-Hall, Inc., *Englewood Cliffs, New Jersey*

13-453431-X

Library of Congress Catalog Card Number 70-101531

Printed in the United States of America

Current printing (last digit):

10   9   8   7   6   5   4   3   2   1

PRENTICE-HALL INTERNATIONAL, INC., London
PRENTICE-HALL OF AUSTRALIA, PTY. LTD., Sydney
PRENTICE-HALL OF CANADA, LTD., Toronto
PRENTICE-HALL OF INDIA PRIVATE LTD., New Delhi
PRENTICE-HALL OF JAPAN, INC., Tokyo

Contents

Preface

This manual is designed for preservice and inservice teachers, both elementary and secondary, as an "active" approach to the improvement of teaching. The approach is described as active because the behavior of each laboratory teacher is central to his learning in the laboratory. The teacher will present short lessons to small groups of pupils or colleagues and will participate in evaluative discussions of his lessons. From these experiences the teacher has the opportunity to improve his teaching, not in an abstract way, but in terms of his ability to put new ideas into practice in the laboratory. The laboratory, particularly when a small group of colleagues works closely together, also presents an opportunity for the teacher to obtain feedback about his ideas, feelings, and patterns of behavior and to provide similar feedback to his colleagues. From these experiences the teacher may increase his sensitivity both to himself and to others and expand his capacity to relate to others in increasingly meaningful ways.

This manual is intended not to be *learned,* but to be *used as a guide* by teachers in experimenting with and improving their teaching. The manual is organized to guide teachers through a cumulative sequence of teaching and learning tasks. Descriptions of the objectives which make up a "task" and alternative strategies for attaining these objectives are presented. Example lessons, evaluative criteria, feedback procedures, and supplementary activities are also included to help illuminate and extend the learnings associated with each task.

Because of the general nature of the teaching and learning tasks of this manual, prospective users should be aware of the broad range of teaching situations to which the manual may be applied. It may be used in introductory educational psychology and curriculum and instruction courses, and in inservice education programs. The wide range of situations to which it is applicable emphasizes the need for appropriate use of the manual. In each situation the needs of the learners and the objectives of the program should be carefully scrutinized and the manual altered, supplemented, or discarded accordingly. In those situations where the manual is used, it should contribute to an involving, active teacher-education program.

A debt of gratitude is due the many preservice and inservice teachers who, through their participation in laboratory experiences with the authors, contributed to the development of this manual. The encouragement given by the Research and Development Center for Teacher Education, The University of Texas at Austin, to the authors' efforts in developing this laboratory approach is sincerely appreciated. It is our hope that users of the manual will continue its development by applying it creatively to their special situations and individual needs.

IMPROVING TEACHING THROUGH EXPERIMENTATION
a laboratory approach

part 1

THE
TEACHING
LABORATORY

chapter 1

The First
Laboratory Lesson

"The next time class meets, you should be prepared to teach a seven-minute lesson to a small group of students." With an introduction such as this, your laboratory experience has begun. The first assignment is simply to teach a short lesson (five to ten minutes) to a small group of your colleagues or pupils (five to eight students). This lesson will not be evaluated on any specific criteria; rather, it will serve to introduce you to the general procedures of the teaching laboratory. This first lesson will also reveal some of your conceptions of what it means "to teach," as well as provide a baseline for determining your progress in the teaching laboratory.

This first lesson is unstructured. You must decide what to teach and how to teach it. You may present, discuss, demonstrate—do anything that you perceive as being appropriate for your students. Because your teaching time is limited, you will need to scale down some aspect of one of your teaching fields. *Don't try to teach too much.* You may ask, "How can anything be taught in seven minutes?" We think you will be surprised at the complex kinds of objectives and strategies that can be utilized in short laboratory lessons when they are carefully designed. Consider how many "long" lessons can be broken down into shorter lessons which, if introduced and concluded appropriately, could stand alone.

It seems inevitable that many of you facing this task will spend a good deal of time, in addition to that spent planning the lesson, simply worrying about how well you will do. It is difficult to predict how things will go during the first lesson. Some teachers will find that they are "out of material" at the end of one minute and will awkwardly conclude, while others will hardly be through their introduction at the end of seven minutes, finding they need at least thirty minutes to finish. Some teachers will become paralyzed with fear before or during their lessons and find that they are unable to go on, while others will be amazed at their unexpected self-confidence and ability to communicate with their pupils.

With effort and the support of their instructor and colleagues, almost all teachers find they can profit from their laboratory experiences. Most teachers who consider their initial lesson a personal disaster soon are achieving successes in the laboratory. Whatever your experiences in this first laboratory lesson, you should try very hard to look at it as merely the first information about you as a teacher—information which you may use to increase self-understanding and to build your teaching competencies.

Since you are not being asked to accomplish a specific objective in this laboratory lesson, no rating scales or observation forms are provided for feedback. We do, however, think it is important that you begin in this lesson to face, to share, and to learn to cope with any anxieties which arise from the challenges of teaching. The following questions may help you and your laboratory colleagues explore these anxieties:

Did you feel anxious before, during, or after your lesson?

Did any specific factors increase or reduce your anxiety?

Can you identify any of the bases of your anxiety?

Was your anxiety due to concern for yourself or for the welfare of your pupils?

How well could you detect anxiety on the part of your colleagues? What can you do to help others reduce or profitably use their anxieties?

What can you do to reduce or profitably use your anxieties?

It is not expected that from this first lesson you will resolve all of the difficult questions posed above. It is only expected that you will begin to use your experiences and the experiences of your colleagues in seeking answers that will, over time, lead to personal growth and an improvement in your ability to teach.

THE FIRST LABORATORY LESSON: SUGGESTED ACTIVITIES

1. In following up your first laboratory lesson, you might also ask the following questions:

How did your students react to you? Did you appear hostile, friendly, fearful, distant?

How did your students react to your lesson?

Was it clear to your students what they were supposed to accomplish from the lesson?

What assumptions were made by you about different students' attitudes and prior knowledge that were important for the success of your lesson?

Were your students interested in your lesson? Did you deliberately attempt to provoke interest?

Did you find out if anything was learned as a result of your lesson?

2. Prior to your first lesson, your group might participate in activities that will help group members get to know one another, for example, your group might participate in an informal discussion of some aspect of teaching.

3. The first laboratory lessons might be followed up by a discussion of the different conceptions of teaching represented by the lessons of each laboratory teacher. Additional input to this discussion might include having each group member draw a picture of himself teaching a class. Such drawings will usually produce a most varied collection of classroom scenes which cast the teacher in very different roles.

4. If your school has a collection of teaching materials, you might examine and draw from them for your first lesson.

5. Readings from the following books may be used in conjunction with your first laboratory lesson and throughout your laboratory experiences. These books have been found particularly provocative in raising questions related to self-understanding.

Perceiving, Behaving, Becoming, 1962 Yearbook. Washington, D.C.: Association for Supervision and Curriculum Development, National Education Association.

Burkhart, R.C., and H.M. Neil, *Identity and Teacher Learning.* Scranton, Pa.: International Textbook Company, 1968.

Jersild, A.T., *When Teachers Face Themselves.* New York: Columbia University, Teachers College Press, 1955.

6. Keeping a diary of thoughts and feelings about oneself and teaching has been found by many teachers to be a useful experience. The diary might include comments on the laboratory or related teaching experiences, on books and articles, and on personal relationships. Your diary may be strictly personal or you may want your instructor or a colleague to react continually to what you write.

chapter 2

The Laboratory Approach

The purpose of this chapter is to help you become familiar with certain characteristics of laboratory teaching. We will discuss five aspects of the laboratory that will be important to you as you begin work on specific teaching activities: (1) the laboratory setting, (2) roles in the laboratory, (3) the teaching and learning tasks presented in later chapters, (4) types of learning that occur in the laboratory, and (5) varieties of feedback.

THE LABORATORY SETTING

Laboratory teaching is unique in that it permits a high degree of control. Lab teaching is *real* teaching, but time, tasks, procedures, pupils, and feedback can all be varied to accommodate any given purpose. Control can be exerted by both the laboratory teacher and the instructor. Such control should increase the chances that learning about teaching is individualized—with success being maximized and failure being an experience from which one can learn rather than an experience one has to live with. While the idea underlying the teaching laboratory is that of learning from experience, it is not a "sink or swim" philosophy; it is a philosophy of controlling experience to maximize desired learning.

The actual physical setting of the teaching laboratory can take a variety of forms. It may be a regular classroom, a small seminar room, one corner of a classroom, or even a small blocked-off space in a hallway. All of these "spaces" have been used as teaching laboratories, and it is anticipated that really adequate facilities will be the exception rather than the rule. For an inservice, school-based laboratory, the regular school classrooms may be utilized.

A space large enough for six to ten pupils and a laboratory teacher has been found to be sufficient for many purposes. Ideally the lab should be equipped with such basic teaching aids as a blackboard, bulletin board, picture hangers, and an overhead projector and screen. Such equipment as record players, tape recorders, and slide, film-strip, and opaque projectors might be made available, along with a teaching materials resource and production center. What is sufficient, of course, depends upon a number of factors: the number of pupils and observers being used, the varieties of teaching equipment being utilized, and the requirements of particular lessons.

Some teachers will prefer specialized environments for their lab lessons such as a gymnasium, science laboratory, or stage. Other teachers will wish to take their groups outside for observation or for physical education activities. Rather than thinking of the teaching laboratory as a particular facility, you are encouraged to make use of the widest possible appropriate teaching environments for your laboratory lessons.

In addition to space and equipment, the laboratory should contain the "raw materials" of teaching—that is, pupils. Using colleagues as pupils is one possibility. Depending upon availability, groups of real pupils may be brought to the teaching laboratory, or the laboratory to the pupils. Feedback and evaluation can be provided by colleagues, pupils, observers, and instructor through the use of evaluation forms, discussion, and audio or video taped recordings of laboratory teaching. Facilities for viewing and listening are necessary when audio and video tape feedback equipment are utilized.

The instructor of a class of thirty or more students or a workshop director in charge of the instruction of a large number of teachers will need to break these large groups into smaller lab groups of seven to ten. Ideally the instructor will have assistants (probably students or teachers who have previously participated in a laboratory) to work with each lab group. An instructor working alone with several lab groups may schedule them at different times or use audio or video tapes of lessons for groups that he cannot work with directly, using group discussions and individual meetings for feedback. An alternative is to structure self-direction by the members of the lab groups while the instructor rotates from group to group.

There are a number of ways that lab groups can be organized. Groups may be formed to meet particular needs so that, for example, teachers of a single subject can work together. Or when the instructor wishes to have all lab teachers exposed to a maximum number of different teaching fields, groups can be so formed. Over time, the composition of lab groups also can be altered for different purposes, but we should mention that having the same individuals work together for several teaching tasks is beneficial. This allows feedback to be based on both immediate and past performance, thereby providing more accurate information for the teacher. Having the same pupils for several lessons also gives the teacher the opportunity to build lessons on prior experiences and discovered pupil needs.

LABORATORY ROLES

When we speak of "a role," we mean those behaviors that are characteristic of some person or group. A role definition may be very general; for instance, if you are asked to play the role of a pupil for a colleague's biology lesson, it simply means that you will be a student during the lesson. It does not mean that you will attempt to behave as would a tenth grade student, with certain understandings and misunderstandings about biology; although if you have not studied biology recently, your knowledge of this subject might not be far from the hypothetical student's.

Of course, we might define a role very specifically. For example, someone might be asked to role-play a 15 year old boy whose behavior in a classroom is characterized as approximately 10 percent aggressive, 40 percent resistant, 30 percent attentive, and 20 percent withdrawn. We might further specify the conditions under which different types of behavior would occur. You should remember that a role is only as specific as its definition and your own experience make it.

The primary role that you will assume in the laboratory is that of teacher. This only means that you will prepare lessons in which you apply certain principles and will attempt to facilitate the learning of your students. Of course, the requirements of particular teaching tasks will put certain constraints on your behavior. The point we wish to make about the teaching role in the lab is that it is usually general.

A consequence of this is that there are many unspecified aspects of your role that you will need to fill in. It will be natural for you to do so by modeling your teaching behavior after that of other teachers you have observed. Ultimately, however, teaching behavior should become a function of what helps students learn rather than what is familiar or secure. The emphasis, therefore, should be on experimenting with your teaching and determining its effects on your students, rather than on trying to fit into some mold already cast by preceding teachers you have observed. When you want to try out some new behaviors or a strategy different from what you have observed to be typical teaching, by all means do so. You will at least be able to get feedback about its effect from your instructor, colleagues and pupils.

Two other important roles, that of pupil and of observer, exist in the laboratory. These roles can be structured in a variety of ways to serve different purposes and to enhance desired learnings. The pupil and observer roles offer significant opportunities for learning and are also vehicles for enhancing the learnings of the lab teachers.

The pupil role may be filled either by real pupils or by you and your colleagues. Both of these groups may be allowed to be "themselves," or they may be asked (or in some cases allowed) to create specified kinds of disturbances in the lab. They can be trained (and this will in most cases be a necessity) to use evaluative instruments and to provide feedback in desired ways: for example, by attending specifically to the stated criteria for evaluating lesson effectiveness. Colleagues can also be trained to role-play different pupil roles. You may view films of pupils and visit classrooms in order to learn to play particular roles. You can demonstrate your knowledge of pupils by behaving as a pupil in the laboratory.

If real pupils are used in the laboratory, colleagues may serve as observers. In the absence of real pupils, some colleagues may assume observer roles while others play pupil roles.

The observer is defined as a nonparticipant in the lesson. He can provide special kinds of feedback, such as continuous written feedback following the same criteria the pupils will use when the lesson is completed. He can learn to use observational systems, focusing his attention on teacher or pupil behavior, or systems which require the quantification of interaction behavior, providing an assessment of classroom climate, amount of teacher-talk, etc. Observational systems considered relevant to specific lab tasks are presented in certain of the task sections in the manual.

In addition to opportunities for learning about techniques of teaching, the laboratory roles of pupil and observer provide the opportunity for a great deal of learning about subject matter. Through the lessons of his colleagues, a teacher in the lab will learn about the substance of his own and other school subjects. Disputes about the value of a teacher's subject will naturally arise out of the laboratory. Teachers will often find they need to justify their subjects and objectives. Often appreciation for the objectives of other teachers and other fields will result from this interaction. These learnings may be viewed as incidental, or they can supplement similar substantive learnings being taught beyond the framework of the lab, such as knowledge of content areas.

We would also like to add a few words about another role that will be important to you in your laboratory experience, that of the instructor. His function will be very diverse. For example, he will decide how much time should be spent on the various tasks and whether all the tasks should be dealt with; he will also be responsible for supplying much of the supplementary material, ideas, instruction, new strategies, and demonstration lessons. During your lesson he may serve as a pupil, an observer, or a supervisor. Most importantly, he will establish the conditions under which you receive feedback about your teaching. Many of the decisions about these activities can be aided by your own perceptions of your progress. (This is one of the aims in education—that the learner can monitor his own performance.) Thus, if you think you need additional instruction on, for instance, the task of motivating, your opinion, if expressed, will play a part in the instructor's decision. The point that we make here is that instructors need feedback from their students, and not just at the end of a course when it is too late to be of benefit to the student.

LABORATORY TASKS

This manual is organized around a series of teaching and learning tasks. A task refers to a distinct objective and appropriate strategies for achieving that objective. Objectives and relevant strategies are of two types—teaching tasks and learning tasks. The teaching tasks developed separately in the next four chapters are:

1. Determining Readiness: determining the aspects of student ability and attitudes relevant to achieving certain learning objectives.

2. Clarifying Objectives: clarifying what is expected of students in terms of what performances are desired.

3. Motivating: providing conditions such that students will be interested in the learning activities and objectives.

4. Evaluating: finding out how well instruction has helped students achieve the objectives of a lesson.

As you progress through the four basic teaching tasks, you will find that we view them as cumulative. That is, after you have taught a lesson focused on the task of determining readiness, you will not abandon that task in your next lesson which concentrates on a new task. Rather, you will attend to the prior task as well as to the new task. For example, in the next laboratory lesson you are to work on determining readiness. In the following lesson, when the task is clarifying objectives, determining readiness becomes a secondary task in that lesson. Likewise, each lesson has a new focus, but other, prior tasks are still relevant and should be attended to. Fortunately, you will find that many of the strategies (e.g. questioning) for accomplishing one teaching task are also useful for other tasks. By the time you have completed the four teaching tasks, you will be attending to them in an integrated way within the same lesson.

The second series of tasks presented in the manual (chapters 7 through 10) are defined as learning tasks. These tasks are differentiated from one another and from the teaching tasks by involving different kinds of learning objectives. As with the teaching tasks, certain kinds of strategies are appropriate to the learning objectives of each learning task. The learning tasks are:

1. Concepts and principles
2. Problem-solving
3. Attitudes
4. Skills

These four categories represent one way (a fairly common one) of viewing the different types of learning that occur in the classroom.

The tasks are not intended to replace instruction in the methods of teaching particular subjects. It is our view that teaching toward these general learning objectives will make your subsequent work on methods more meaningful, since you will have acquired a general perspective of your subject.

Although presented separately, the learning tasks are built on the teaching tasks, since each learning task can be analyzed in terms of the teaching tasks. For example, the following questions are relevant to concept learning:

1. What abilities, interests, and previous knowledge are necessary for learning a particular concept? (Determining Readiness)

2. What does "learning" a particular concept mean in terms of expected pupil behavior? (Clarifying Objectives)

3. How can students be motivated to learn a particular concept? (Motivating)

4. How can the learning of a concept be determined? (Evaluating)

Teaching each of the learning tasks, will, therefore, involve the teaching tasks. In a final chapter we will ask you to generate a learning task based on some other conceptualization of types of learning.

A LABORATORY VIEWPOINT OF "TEACHING"

Viewing teaching as comprised of tasks—objectives and appropriate strategies— emphasizes the role of the teacher as that of a decision maker, a designer of instruction, a hypothesis generator and tester. The presentation in this manual encourages a view of the teacher as one continuously searching for answers to the question: "What procedures, under what conditions, and for what kinds of pupils, are effective in achieving various types of student learning?"

The decision-making functions of the teacher will unfold with the specification of each of the teaching and learning tasks. The basic notion in each task situation is that you must choose from among alternate strategies in attempting to achieve the task objective. A choice of strategy represents a hypothesis; the application of the strategy represents its test. All strategy tests result in evidence on which to base new strategy selection and implementation. No test is conclusive because you cannot rule out the effects of many variables contributing to a particular outcome and because new conditions will likely be present when the strategy is again employed. As a result of these complexities, you will engage in never-ending accumulation of evidence on which to base future decisions about teaching.

In addition to emphasis on the view of teaching as decision-making, we stress a second view in this manual: teaching, in addition to comprising the effective use of strategies, involves the ability to communicate, to relate, to empathize with your students. This second view is not entirely distinct from the first. For example, the task of determining readiness emphasizes finding out about pupils. Yet, this view of the teacher as an effective communicator is sufficiently important in and of itself to merit some separate treatment.

Therefore, some of the activities presented at the end of each teaching and learning task chapter are an attempt to encourage development of communication skills. These activities are based on the assumption that learning in this domain involves learning to accept yourself, becoming concerned less with yourself and more with your pupils, and increasing your understanding of the ideas and feelings of others. Your experiences in laboratory teaching will provide you with feedback about your ability to communicate with others.

FEEDBACK IN THE LABORATORY

Obtaining information about what you do as a teacher that is effective, ineffective, or in-between, and why, is certainly necessary for your continuing to improve as a teacher.

One way to learn about yourself as a teacher is through feedback (from your instructor, colleagues, and students) about your behavior and its effects on the students you teach. Feedback provides another source of information with which you can check out your perceptions; without it you would have to rely solely on your own perceptions of the effects of your teaching. Feedback can suggest which behaviors you need to modify, to eliminate, or to continue practicing. Feedback provides a way to find out why an objective you tried to teach was not reached, and it can help you to understand why a strategy you tried was particularly effective. Therefore, it is very important that provision be made for some type of feedback and that you contribute your perceptions, both negative and positive, of your colleagues' teaching in the laboratory.

There are basically two types of feedback: descriptive and evaluative. The former type is an attempt to recreate for the teacher the behavior observed during the lesson, with no attempt to judge the adequacy of the performance; the intent is simply to describe, in some way, what the teacher and the class did. Evaluative feedback implies a comparison to some criterion. The criterion may be highly value-laden and nonspecific ("good" vs. "bad"). It may be abstract (the "ideal" teacher), or concrete (your previous lesson). The difference between descriptive and evaluative feedback may be seen by comparing the statements "He praised student performance six times," and "For the purposes of this lesson, he praised too often (or too little)." There is a place for both types of feedback in the laboratory, and, in general, they will serve complementary purposes.

Feedback can be aided by *rating scales* and by *observation forms.* Both kinds of instruments require an observer and/or pupil to report back to the teacher certain kinds of behavior relevant for the teaching task. These instruments, as feedback devices, will serve several purposes. They will focus attention on relevant dimensions of behavior, provide more standardized feedback conditions across laboratory groups, and allow the teacher to note his progress over time on the several teaching task dimensions.

Rating Scales

There are several kinds of ratings that can be used in the laboratory:

1. A pupil can rate the effect of instruction on himself ("I was very interested in the lesson").
2. A pupil or observer can rate the adequacy of the instruction itself ("The teacher used an appropriate motivating strategy very effectively").
3. An observer can rate the effect of a lesson on the pupils ("The pupils appeared very interested in the lesson").

Of these three kinds of ratings, the first type, a pupil rating of the effect of instruction on himself, will be utilized in this manual. Each teaching and learning task will be accompanied by a rating scale relevant to that dimension. The ratings should be made by students as soon as the lesson is completed and accompanied by comments describing the basis for the rating, as well as suggestions for improving the lesson.

Other types of ratings, when appropriate, may be used. If there are observers, ratings of the effect of the lesson on the pupils might be useful for providing a comparison with the pupils' own ratings. Rating the adequacy of some aspect of instruction itself may be helpful, if the rater is trying to provide feedback about an aspect of teaching which is independent of the particular pupils (e.g., voice projection, shifting the focus of the lesson, eye contact, etc.).

For example, the teaching task labeled "Motivating" is accompanied by the following rating scale:

Were you interested in the lesson?
1. Intensely interested
2. Considerably interested
3. Generally interested; sometimes disinterested
4. Somewhat interested
5. Very little interested
6. Not interested at all

The pupils (or colleagues acting as pupils) are asked to judge their own interest in the lesson. Thus, as the teacher you would receive several separate ratings of interest. These ratings are valuable and would allow you to check the accuracy of your own evaluation of student interest. From these ratings you have some basis for judging the effectiveness of a motivating strategy you might have tried in the lesson.

Some information is not contained in the ratings, but may be obtained from a discussion of them. In this case, the reasons for high and low ratings of interest appear to be most important, since your future choice of a motivating strategy may be more appropriate if you understand the effects on different pupils of what you have done. A discussion of why a particular strategy might work for one set of pupils but not another may serve to remind you of individual differences and the necessity for variety in your teaching. Likewise, you would no doubt appreciate receiving suggestions for alternative strategies, as well as reinforcement for effective behavior.

One reason for differences in ratings of the same lesson will be the differential effect of a strategy on the raters. What interests one pupil may bore another. These differences should stimulate discussion and promote greater awareness of the varying effect of different strategies.

However, other reasons for differences in ratings will interfere with the usefulness of ratings as a feedback device. Probably the most troublesome aspect of rating is the difficulty in specifying behavioral referents for the scale. For example, just what does a rating of "considerably interested" mean? Some possible meanings might be:

"I wanted to continue further with the lesson."
"A pupil asks the teacher to suggest further readings in the area."

"Pupils were attentive throughout the lesson."

"Students raised many questions about the content."

Any one or all of these statements might be indicative of "considerably interested" (a rating of 2). The problem, however, is that the statements seem equally capable of representing "intensely interested" (a rating of 1) or possibly "generally interested" (a rating of 3). Moreover, personal definitions of "interest" will vary. By specifying referents for points along a rating scale, it is possible to arrive at a general understanding of what is to be meant by different degrees of "interest," but individuals will still retain idiosyncratic meanings as well, and these will influence the ratings you receive.

There is no really adequate way to eliminate all sources of bias in ratings. They can be reduced, however, in two ways. First, when rating scales are presented, they will be accompanied by referents for each point along the scale. This will help give a common dimension of meaning in the ratings. Second, ratings should be accompanied by comments from the raters, written or oral, which explain the reasons for the ratings. Through this combination of evaluation and description you will obtain more information on which to base future decisions about strategies, as well as a clearer meaning of the given rating.

In the laboratory lesson for the first teaching task, "Determining Readiness," the rating scale used will assess the readiness information obtained by the teacher. In the lesson "Clarifying Objectives" two rating scales will be used, one for the task of determining readiness and another for clarifying objectives, since you should attend to the task of clarifying objectives as well as determining pupil readiness during the second lesson. By the time you have completed the fourth teaching task, four ratings will be in use to assess performance on each of the four teaching tasks. Thus, you will receive feedback about four dimensions of your teaching during the fourth and each subsequent lesson. In practice, it will occasionally be true that some dimensions are less relevant than others for a lesson. In that case, ratings can be made only on relevant tasks. This will be the case particularly when the available time is limited. For example, a lesson dealing with divergent problem-solving may require more time than is available to handle adequately each teaching task as well as carry out a strategy for attaining the learning objective. In order to carry out the lesson within a specified time period (e.g., ten minutes) you might make certain assumptions about pupil readiness and simply not attend to that aspect of teaching during the lesson. You would not, of course, receive a rating on that dimension; but since you would presumably have received feedback about this aspect of your teaching in several previous lessons, the omission of it at this point would not be serious.

Selective use of certain rating scales can help individualize your instruction in the teaching laboratory. After receiving ratings of several lessons you will typically find some variation in your rated performance across task dimensions. Thus, you may find your ratings on "Clarity" and "Determining Readiness" high, whereas those on "Motivating" may be low. You might profitably concentrate your efforts on improving performance on the poorly rated dimension, even if it means attending less to the more highly rated dimensions. An attempt to individualize instruction will require that both you and your instructor periodically review the cumulative ratings.

One aspect of feedback, then, will be pupil or observer ratings relevant to the particular teaching task. These ratings will provide continuity to the laboratory experience, since succeeding lessons will incorporate ratings of previously experienced instructional dimensions. Ratings are accompanied by written comments and discussion, elaborating on and clarifying the meaning of the rating and providing criticism as well as support along with suggestions for improvement.

Figures 1 and 2 present summary sheets which may be used to keep a record of your performance on both the teaching and learning tasks in the laboratory. For each lesson space is provided for a record of the colleagues' or pupils' ratings, as well as the instructor's.

In summary, these rating scales have several uses as feedback tools. They provide an assessment of important aspects of instruction; they lend continuity to the laboratory and provide you with a record of performance (as perceived by raters) across a series of lessons, thus highlighting areas of strength and areas needing more work; and they should also serve as a starting point for discussion of your teaching behavior as observed in the laboratory.

Observation Forms

Observation forms are used to summarize the behavior of the teacher and/or pupils during a lesson. That is, certain behaviors are identified as important; the observer's task is simply to note the frequency of occurrence of each of them. One of the differences between an observation form and a rating scale is that the rating scale always involves some kind of judgment or comparison to a criterion, whereas the observation form requires only a decision on whether the behavior is an instance of a particular category.

For example, suppose you were interested in the amount of teacher-talk as compared to student-talk during one of your lessons. An observation form would require simply that an observer keep track of the amount of teacher-talk and student-talk (using a stop watch or making a tally mark every three or five seconds, for example) and compute the ratio of one to the other.

On the other hand, a rating scale may require the observer to evaluate some aspect of the lesson.

During the lesson, the teacher, compared with the students, talked
1. Too much
2. A little too much
3. About the right amount
4. Not quite enough
5. Not nearly enough

Figure 1

SUMMARY RATING FORM: TEACHING TASK LESSONS

Lesson Sequence	DETERMINING READINESS		CLARITY		MOTIVATION		EVALUATION	
	coll/pup. Colleague	instr/obs. Instructor	coll/pup. Colleague	instr/obs. Instructor	coll/pup. Colleague	instr/obs. Instructor	coll/pup. Colleague	instr/obs. Instructor
1. Determining Pupil Readiness			✕	✕	✕	✕	✕	✕
2. Clarifying Instructional Objectives					✕	✕	✕	✕
3. Motivating							✕	✕
4. Evaluating								

Figure 2

SUMMARY RATING FORM: LEARNING TASK LESSONS

Lesson Sequence	ATTAINING LESSON OBJECTIVES		CLARITY		DETERMINING READINESS		MOTIVATING		EVALUATING	
	Coll.	Inst.	Coll.	Inst.	Coll.	Inst.	Coll.	Inst.	Coll.	Inst.
1. Concept or principle learning										
2. Problem-solving										
3. Attitude formation										
4. Skill development										

Use of this rating scale requires the rater to make a judgment about a total lesson. That is, the teacher's behavior over an extended period of time must be remembered and rated. In contrast, the observation procedure described above requires continuous recording of behavior, so that smaller segments of behavior are noted as they occur, and little reliance is placed on memory.

An Example of an Observation Form

A very simple observation form is represented by the frequency of behavior of two categories: teacher-talk (TT) and student-talk (ST). An observer would simply sit in on a lesson and tally the verbal behavior of the participants. Of course, the teacher, for self-analysis, could listen to a tape recording of his lesson and code it himself.

Suppose an observer were coding behavior every three seconds, and he observed a lesson containing the following verbal behavior:

		Code*
Teacher:	(Yesterday we learned that different kinds of stone	T.T.
	could be formed) (in many ways. Can anyone	T.T.
	remember what those ways were?)	
Student:	(By heat. Like if heat melts different things and they	S.T.
	run together.)	
Teacher:	(Good. When it cools, then there is a stone with	T.T.
	different substances in it.)	
Student:	(Pressure is another way. If two things are pushed	S.T.
	together they can fuse.)	

*Code mark indicates the appropriate category for each segment, the parentheses indicating an utterance of approximately three seconds' duration.

An observation form for this brief interchange would show three tallies for teacher-talk and two tallies for student-talk, since approximately nine seconds and six seconds were used for teacher- and student-talk respectively.

Category	Tallies
Teacher-Talk	///
Student-Talk	//

If a whole lesson were coded in this way, the only question that could be answered would be: What percentage of the time did the teacher or the students talk? This would be useful information if you were concerned with the amount of student participation in your lesson.

Suppose, however, you were interested in the frequency of positive reinforcement you used during a lesson and in what kind of student behavior you reinforced. The following observation form could be used.

Student Behavior	Teacher's Frequency of Reinforcement
States fact	
States opinion	
Asks question	
Other	

Assuming that these types of student behavior were important (others could be substituted, of course), and that they, as well as positively reinforcing teacher behavior, had been defined, the observer would check the appropriate category whenever the teacher reinforced student behavior. The observation record of the lesson would provide information about the relative frequency of reinforcement used by the teacher for the different student behaviors. If you also wanted to know how often you did *not* reinforce pupil behavior, the observer could use, instead of a check mark, a plus (+) for each occurrence of a reinforcing statement and a zero (0) for each instance of a verbal behavior that was not reinforced. The table below shows such an observation form resulting from a discussion.

Student Behavior	Teacher's Frequency of Reinforcement/Nonreinforcement
States fact	++++00+00+0+0+++
States opinion	0+000
Asks question	000
Other	0+0

Information available from this observation form indicates that the predominant mode of student behavior was stating facts.[1] The teacher reinforced this student behavior frequently (almost two-thirds of the time) and initially reinforced this behavior each time it occurred.

In addition, the teacher tended not to reinforce opinions and questions from the students (one might speculate that this was one reason for the low incidence of these behaviors compared to "student states facts"). We cannot say how appropriate the teacher's behavior was, since that depends on the purpose of the

[1]Note that the unit of observation is the occurrence of a behavior; that is, the observer only records whether the teacher behavior occurred or did not occur subsequent to the student behavior. In the previous example of an observation form (teacher- and student-talk) the observation unit was a time period, three seconds.

lesson, but we do have an objective record of what could be very relevant for a lesson. It is a type of feedback that can suggest what direction modification of behavior should take, since it specifies very clearly the answers to certain questions about teacher and student behavior.

Observation forms are provided in many of the chapters of this manual. They are intended to be used to provide objective feedback about particular aspects of teacher and student behavior in the lessons you teach. You may use observation forms for self-analysis from a video or audio tape recording of your lessons, or colleagues may use an observation form to record behavior during your lesson.

The observation forms presented in this manual have been developed so that they can be used after one-half hour to an hour's practice. Roughly 70 percent agreement between observers during practice is generally satisfactory to produce meaningful information.

To compute the percentage agreement for a single category, you may use the following formula:[2]

$$\text{Agreement} = 1 - \frac{A - B}{A + B}$$

where (A-B) is the difference between two observers' tallies (with A being the larger number); and (A + B) is the sum of the observers' tallies. For example, if observer A has 14 tallies in a category and observer B has 10, then the percentage of observer agreement is:

$$1 - \frac{14 - 10}{14 + 10} = 1 - \frac{4}{24} = 1 - (.17)$$

$$1 - (.17) = .83 \text{ or } 83\% \text{ agreement}$$

Several persons might be assigned the role of observer for a particular task, and the observer role rotated to different colleagues for new tasks. In this way, no one person will need to learn to code using all forms. Thus, you will learn to code behavior using an observation system only when you are in the role of an observer or when you code your own lesson for analysis. Learning the observation system will be facilitated by lessons provided in the chapters. These are coded in order to provide examples of behaviors on the observation forms.

Before using an observation form you should ascertain whether the procedure will provide relevant feedback. Although we have designed the forms presented with the instructional tasks to provide information appropriate to important aspects of each task, we have by no means delineated all important behaviors. To do so would necessitate very complex instruments requiring much training time.

Consequently, when using a form for self-coding your own lesson, you may wish to alter existing categories to capture behaviors more appropriate to your objectives. You may also disregard an observation form entirely when other types of descriptive feedback are more meaningful. Usually, however, you will

---

[2]This procedure assumes that the best estimate of the "true" number of tallies in a category is the average of the two observers' estimates.

find that the objective description of your teaching behavior provided by an observation form is a very useful aid for analyzing your teaching and for suggesting alternative modes of behavior.

THE LABORATORY APPROACH: SUGGESTED ACTIVITIES

1. For a valuable supplement to your laboratory experiences, you might observe teachers and students in a variety of educational settings, for example, university classes, elementary and secondary school classes, and adult vocational classes. Use the laboratory tasks as one frame of reference for describing and evaluating your observations.

2. Many preservice teachers have found tutoring to be a valuable supplement to their laboratory experiences as well as a rewarding teaching experience. You might choose to tutor through a voluntary tutoring program, if one is active in your community.

3. Preservice teachers may find that serving as a classroom teacher's assistant, particularly when opportunities to teach are involved, can be a valuable teacher preparation experience. The learnings of the lab and the assistant experience will allow you to apply teaching strategies in different settings. (Of course this experience depends upon the cooperation of a school system and classroom teachers.)

4. T-group experiences may be developed along with the experiences of the teaching laboratory to increase communication among individuals. For background information on T-group procedures refer to, *T-Group Theory and Laboratory Method* by Leland P. Bradford, Jack R. Gibb, and Kenneth D. Benne, New York: John Wiley and Sons, Inc., 1964.

5. For another perspective on the teaching laboratory, particularly information on laboratory applications and teaching skills, refer to *Microteaching* by Dwight Allen and Kevin Ryan, Reading, Mass.: Addison-Wesley, 1969.

part 2

BASIC
TEACHING TASKS

The next four chapters focus on four basic teaching tasks:

1. Determining Readiness
2. Clarifying Objectives
3. Motivating
4. Evaluating

These tasks represent a model of teaching, that is, one way to break the complex process of teaching into separate parts. The model should be useful in that it indicates components which you may practice in developing teaching skills. In addition it will give you a framework from which to generate teaching strategies.

The tasks of the model are presented in a particular order, but they are interrelated. For example, the objectives of instruction are in part a function of the readiness of students, but the aspects of readiness that you will seek to determine are in turn dependent upon the objectives. The information gained by evaluating progress toward some objective will influence the nature of subsequent objectives, in addition to influencing the types of motivating strategies you use, and so on.

Chapter 3 starts with the task of determining readiness, and the subsequent chapters in Part II are developed cumulatively, each building on the previous tasks. When you reach the last task you will have completed the teaching model, and you will have arrived back at the beginning. The tasks are aspects of a cycle of activities which, when combined with the learning tasks presented in Part III, constitute one way of viewing the process of teaching.

chapter 3

Determining Readiness

OBJECTIVE

In your first laboratory lesson the chances are that you delivered a presentation which allowed for little or no pupil response. You thought of your lesson more as a performance than as an opportunity actually to teach something to someone. Whether your pupils already knew what you were teaching probably was not of major concern to you. For example, you may have said, "Pretend you are just beginning to learn Spanish." This may have been good coping behavior for the first lesson, but the fact is that the statement indicates more concern for your own survival than for the students' learning. Also, you may have made some assumptions about the attitudes, interests, and understandings of your pupils. For example, you may have begun by saying, "Let's assume you are all interested in history and we have just finished studying World War I." Although there was nothing wrong with making these assumptions in the first lesson, you cannot go on in this manner forever. Sooner or later you will find out the extent of student interest in history and how much was retained from the study of World War I, and whether these are sufficient to proceed as you originally intended.

Your task for this lesson is to determine readiness. Rather than being responsible for "teaching something" you are responsible for "learning something." You are responsible for learning as much as you can about the characteristics of your pupils which you determine are relevant to what you want to teach. Subject matter for this lesson may be thought of very generally—for example, American history; or it may be quite specific—for example, interpreting the first line of the Declaration of Independence. In other words, for this lesson you may choose to explore your pupils' readiness to learn in a very general sense or you may explore readiness relative to quite specific objectives. In either case, you are not responsible for using the information which you gain in any particular way, for example, to restructure your lesson;

you are responsible only for generating information about your pupils which is relevant to your subject matter or to a particular objective.

We do not mean to imply that it is unimportant to make use of the information you obtain in determining readiness. However, most of the remaining instructional and learning tasks will assume that you obtain information about student readiness and proceed from that point, so in this lesson you need only be concerned with obtaining readiness information.

It is helpful to think of readiness as consisting of many characteristics, each characteristic having degrees of readiness. In an algebra class, for instance, a teacher will be interested, before teaching his class how to solve systems of simultaneous equations, in knowing to what extent students can state the meaning of certain symbols and terms, and how well students can graph and solve simple equations. Important also will be the attitudes of the students toward algebra, whether they see any relevance of the topic to other goals they may have, and their expectations of success in the class. Information about student readiness on these characteristics will be useful to the teacher in making decisions about what objectives are realistic for different students, and what kinds of instructional and motivational strategies might be most effectively employed. Making these instructional decisions in view of readiness information will be among your most difficult and challenging teaching problems.

STRATEGIES FOR DETERMINING READINESS

It is useful to think of using strategies for determining readiness at two different times during the lesson: prior to and concurrent with instruction. Often before you ever begin to teach toward an objective, you will use questions, tests, observations, and other strategies to determine student knowledge and interest. Then, when you are in the process of teaching something, you will be continually gaining information about the readiness of your pupils.

An example of determining readiness prior to and concurrent with instruction is provided by a science teacher who takes his class outside to collect samples of plant life, the ultimate objective being for the student to classify his plants into categories. As the teacher interacts with his pupils about their plants, he can observe their reactions and from them determine which characteristics of the plants are attended to, and thus be prepared to direct attention to unnoticed attributes important for the desired classification.

For your lesson on determining readiness you may choose to use strategies for gaining information from your pupils prior to and/or concurrent with instruction.

Observation of Performance as a Strategy for Determining Readiness

This strategy for determining readiness comprises many activities, most of which are based on observing pupil performance on tasks relevant to the instructional objectives.

All subjects have particular kinds of performances which are expected when a part of the subject is learned. You may select one or more performances which you consider important and from which you might be able to decide what learning objectives are most appropriate for different pupils. These performances may involve written and oral exercises. For example, in order to determine the extent to which students can clearly express their impressions or feelings, an English teacher could ask his pupils to write their interpretations of a popular song, or he could ask that they express orally the feelings which the music aroused in them.

Another kind of performance consists of responding to various kinds of written test items. A mathematics teacher, for instance, could begin a lesson on sets by giving a short quiz which calls for identification of concepts needed to learn about sets.

Listening and oral performances will be particularly important to most foreign language teachers. Thus, a Spanish teacher might begin her lesson by seeing how well her pupils can repeat different sounds of the language.

Observing performances will also be important to many other subject areas. For example, a physical education teacher can gain considerable information about the abilities of his students by observing them during some sports activity. He will also gain some understanding of individual students' attitudes toward cooperation and competition. An art teacher could have her pupils try their hand at leather carving or painting. A home economics teacher might give her pupils parts of a dress pattern to see if they could correctly cut out their pieces of material. An industrial arts teacher could ask his pupils to tell what they know about the operation of a gasoline engine.

It is important to note that many types of performance are relevant to every subject area, and the examples above should not limit the kinds of performances in which you are interested. For example, oral and written test items are means of assessing readiness in most subject areas. Also, careful observation of pupils while they are attempting to perform a specified task may give you considerable information about their attitudes toward the particular task.

If you decide to try this strategy, you need to develop an activity requiring student behavior relevant to those aspects of readiness that you wish to assess. You should then observe student performance during the activity (or after the activity, if a written performance is required), to determine the individual pupils' various states of readiness.

Questions as a Strategy for Determining Readiness

Questions serve many purposes, but one of the results of all questions (except rhetorical questions) is that they result in information. Thus pupils' responses (or lack of responses) provide a good source for determining readiness. Questions may be designed specifically for the purpose of determining readiness, and such questions should be planned to obtain a maximum of relevant information.

The first aspect of questioning that you should consider is content. Will your questions elicit factual responses, applications, interpretations, or evaluations?

Or will they stimulate expressions of feelings and opinions? If you wish to determine whether students can state specific facts, then obviously you need to ask only factual questions. However, if you wish to determine the students' ability to interpret some event or to use a concept to differentiate among certain examples, you must do more than simply ask for a description of the event or a definition of the concept. Your question should require interpretation or application.

As self-evident as the previous paragraph may seem, formulating questions beyond the factual level requires considerable skill. Therefore, if you plan to use questioning to determine readiness, you should develop questions beforehand that indeed match the type of understanding that you wish to assess.

A second aspect of questioning to consider is how to guide and maintain discussion or interaction. Often a student response will not provide sufficient information, and never can one infer from a single student's response the understanding possessed by the rest of the class. Also if a discussion becomes complex, or if a student's response has strayed from the content of the question, some confusion may occur. Consequently, some additional questioning strategies are important.

   1.   You can ask pupils to *extend* their responses: "Can you add to that?" "Can you explain that more fully?"
   2.   You can ask for *clarification*: "What do you mean by that?" "Would you rephrase that?"
   3.   You can challenge pupils to *justify* what they have said: "Why do you say that?" "What reason or evidence can you give to support that idea?"
   4. I You can bring in new pupils by *directing* a question to other pupils: "John, do you agree with that?"
   5.   You can ask pupils to *summarize* what has been said: "It sounds as if there have been several viewpoints expressed thus far. Could someone summarize these for us?"

Thus, if you use questioning to determine readiness, you should not only consider the content of the question you will ask, but also ways to guide and maintain the interaction resulting from the questioning.

Related to questioning is the ability to use silence. If you ask a question and if no answer is immediately forthcoming, just relax and carefully observe your students. You may detect from quizzical expressions that you were not understood. You may see signs that a student wants to answer but needs to be personally called upon. While observing you may think of hints or ways to clarify your question. Often the silence will provoke a response because it shows that you intend an answer or because it gives students time to think. Be attentive to the power of silence to elicit information from your students.

The above strategies are those you might draw upon in attempting to determine readiness. Of course you need not attempt to use all of these in your lesson. Rather, in view of the information which you hope to gain, you should choose those strategies which you think will achieve success. From this first determining readiness lesson, you will gain information about those you teach and about your own performance, which should better help you select strategies in the subsequent lessons.

In actual practice, the assessment of readiness in a classroom is a continuing process. The more one interacts with students, observes them, reads their papers, etc., the more one acquires insight into their motives and abilities and hence, their readiness for new learning. In this laboratory lesson, you should try to elicit as much as possible those pupil responses and behaviors relevant to your subject in general or your lesson objectives in particular.

In preparing for this lesson, you will find it helpful to list relevant aspects of behavior or student characteristics. For example, aspects of readiness for a science lesson in which the objective is to learn the concept of osmosis might include knowledge of concepts and principles necessary to learn this particular concept (e.g., permeability), interest in this and related topics, and attitudes toward science. In preparing for a unit on poetry, and depending on what you wish to accomplish, you may be interested in your students' understanding of and attitude toward different kinds of poetry, their knowledge of different forms of poetic expression, their prior experiences with poetry, whether they can state different levels of meaning of oral and written expression, what kinds of poetry interests them, etc.

To summarize, once you have delineated one or more important behaviors or characteristics, you can plan procedures whereby you determine student readiness on these characteristics.

These procedures, or strategies, include:

1. Specifying an activity for students to perform so that you may observe their performance. Included in this strategy are oral and written performances, as well as psychomotor activities.

2. Plan a discussion based upon questioning. In this strategy you should attend to the content of your questions, as well as to ways of maintaining and guiding the interaction.

Levels of performance for determining readiness are specified on the "Evaluation and Feedback Guide" at the end of the chapter. This Guide can be used by your pupils, observers, and your instructor as one way to provide you with feedback about your lesson. Comments provided on the form should, to some extent, focus on the task of determining readiness, and they should, when possible, give evidence for the numerical evaluation given and provide suggestions for improvement. You can also use the guide in evaluating your own lesson, after you have taught, or from an audio or video recording.

OBSERVATION FORMS FOR DETERMINING READINESS

Use of these observation forms will provide information about one aspect of determining readiness: questioning. Two observation forms are provided.

Form I, Patterns of Interaction, may be used to determine how the questioning procedure is managed. To use this system the observer first must decide whether a teacher question can stand alone (Teacher Question A) or whether it to some extent builds on, uses, or extends a response to a previous question (Teacher Question B). If the question was Type A, then the observer should decide whether the question was addressed to the class in general, or to a specific student; if it was a Type B question, then the observer must decide if it was addressed to the class, the same student who answered the previous question, or to a different student. Whichever category the question belongs to receives a check on the observation form. If the teacher statement was not a question, then a check should be made in the row for "Teacher Statements, Other" (use a check each time a separate idea is expressed).

Student statements are classified according to whether they occur in response to the teacher's question or to another student. If a statement cannot be classified into either of these categories, then it is coded into "Student Statements, Other."

Summary data from this observation sheet will provide the following information about questioning strategies: the number of teacher questions, to whom they were directed, the extent to which the questions built on student responses, and the relative frequency of each category. Categories may be combined to produce other information (e.g., teacher-talk and student-talk).

Form II, Question Content, provides information about three types of content of questions and responses.

1. Facts: This category includes facts, descriptions of events, specific information, and naming or identifying.
2. Preferences: Includes opinions, statements of belief, value, attitude, preference, or interest.
3. Reasons, Inferences: Includes giving reasons, making inferences, drawing conclusions, generalizations, application.

Each teacher question and each student statement is coded (with a check mark) into one of these three broad categories. All other verbal behavior is coded either into "Teacher Statements, Other" or "Student Statements, Other." Summary data from this observation form will specify the amount of the different types of content occurring during the lesson. You, as the teacher, must judge the extent to which the relative frequencies of the behaviors observed during the lesson reflect the content you intended to assess in your determining readiness lesson.

FORM I: PATTERNS OF INTERACTION*

		Code†							
Teacher Questions (A)	To Class	TQA-C							
	To Student	TQA-S							
Teacher Questions (B)	To Class	TQB-C							
	To Same Student	TQB-S¹							
	To New Student	TQB-S²							
Teacher Statements, Other		TSO							
Student Statements	To Teacher	SS-T							
	To Student (s)	SS-S							
Student Statements, Other		SSO							

*Use the blank space in each row to tally.

†The sample lesson (p. 37) is coded using these symbols.

FORM II: QUESTION CONTENT*

		code†	
Teacher Questions	Facts	TQF	
	Preferences	TQP	
	Reasons, Infers	TQR	
Teacher Statements, Other		TSO	
Student Statements	Facts	SSF	
	Preferences	SSP	
	Reasons, Infers	SSR	
Student Statements, Other		SSO	

* Use the blank space in each row to tally.
† The sample lesson (p. 37) is coded using this system.

DETERMINING READINESS:
LESSON FOR ANALYSIS AND EVALUATION

LESSON	Coding		ANALYSIS
	Form I	Form II	
T (teacher): Is everyone familiar with the poetry of John Keats? Can someone give me some impressions of John Keats's poetry? Remember anything you've read by him?	TCA-C TCA-C TQA-C	TQF TQF TQF	Pre-instructional questions— an alternative would be to give more information to en- hance recall prior to asking the questions.
S1 (first student): Sensualism. He went out of his way to express things. . .	SS-T	SSF	
T: That's right. He's very emotional, very sensual. You can almost feel his poetry. Anything else? Barbara?	TSO TQB-C	TSO TQF	
S2: Usually starts with an apostrophe to the gods or. . .	SS-T	SSF	Students express detailed knowledge in a sophisticated way. Teacher seems to be cut-
T: He's very classical in his romanticism. Yes?	TSO	TSO	ting students off and adding information which could be drawn from them.
S3: He wrote a lot of sonnets and he used this classical form in his sonnets.	SS-T	SSF	
T: Right, right. That's fine! I'm glad to know that several of you are acquainted with him. But there is one aspect of Keats that is very important. Before we start reading him, before we even look at his poetry, before we even take up this next week's work with Keats—this is the con- cept called—now don't let this scare you (writing on the blackboard)—it's very easy: *negative capability.* He did quite a bit of work on this, and as a matter of fact, you can find examples of it in just about everything he did. Does anyone have any idea about what this might be? Negative capability? (silence) What about if I say it this way? If I said it was a tangle of inseparable and irreconciliable opposites. Then would you know? Gret- chen?	TSO TSO TSO TSO TQA-C TQA-C	TSO TSO TSO TSO TQF TQR	How many students have this intimate knowledge of Keats? Unfortunate use of "but." Presumes students don't know—minimizes what they do know. Good use of probing, silence, and additional information.
S4: I haven't read anything. But the first thing that comes in my mind is the contradicting things that come into your feelings. For example, feelings of love.	SS-T	SSR	

LESSON	Coding		ANALYSIS
	Form I	Form II	
T: Right. The most—one of the most important points of negative capability is simply this feeling of contradiction. Okay, let's put it down on just an everyday level. Let's say you're running in a contest of some kind and you're running for, oh, some office in school—say, student council president. And it just so happens one of your closest friends is running against you. Okay, now you win the election and you're happy to win. But there is a little element of sadness in this too, because you know this friend very well and he had to lose, and it was sad that you had to run against each other. And so in the joy of winning there was an element of sadness. Right? Can anyone else give me an example from your everyday life of this—this contradicting thing? (silence) What about in death?	TSO TQB-C TQA-C	TSO TQR	Student apparently feels need to express relative lack of knowledge on Keats. Responsive student. This interpretation might have been probed for elaboration and examples. This may indicate an area of meaning for this pupil. Good example by teacher. Good question focusing on possible area of concern to pupils.
S5 When someone dies who's been in pain, you're sorry, sad—you miss them. There's an emptiness. But you're glad it's over for them.	SS-T	SSR	Good response. Student applies concept to his own experience. Now information about pupil readiness is clearly concurrent with process of achieving objectives of lesson. Students are handling this concept very perceptively. Teacher seems to have related discussion to students' interests.
T: Right, so you see, there's this contradiction in just about everything you do.	TSO	TSO	
S6 Sometimes the people you love are the ones you get the most unhappy with because you care more about them.	SS-T	SSR	
T: Right. This is the old thing—that sometimes hate is the closest emotion to love. This happens quite often in Keats. Okay, uh, let's look at some of his poetry. Now, I'm not interested in what the poems mean right now. I'm just interested in phrases illustrating this concept of negative capability. Okay, what about this phrase—(writes on board) *aching pleasure,* what could that mean? Linda?	TSO TSO TSO TSO TQA-C	TSO TQF	
S6: Well, that's back to what I said about love. If you care so much it hurts.	SS-T	SSF	Love seems to be of concern to students.

LESSON	Coding Form I	Coding Form II	ANALYSIS
T: Okay, can you expand this more—in terms of love?	TQB-S$_1$	TQR	Good probe. Teacher picks up the love theme.
S4: It seems that after you finally reach it, you find that it's not what it was—and there's a loneliness. . .	SS-T	SSR	Student continues love theme started earlier. Very sensitive response.
T: That's right, It's almost a letdown. You've striven for a thing; then you are there, and the strife is over with, and there's a tinge of melancholy. Of course, there are many interpretations, but that's a very good one. Bob, did you want to add to that?	TSO TSO TQB-S$_2$	TSO TSO TQP	Would more information from student, possibly an example, have been useful? Additional student brought out.
S7: Oh, I was just going to say I don't think it is as much a letdown as much as you said—more a blending of happiness and melancholy.	SS-T	SSP	
T: Right. Right. This is one of the best things in Keats for me, and I hope it will be for you. This very idea of negative capability—that you can look at his poetry and see so many contradictions. You can see his very belief in life—he had a very short life, but the thing that bothered him his whole life was this problem that he could never really be happy. Every time he felt happiness, he felt pain, and every time he felt pain there was a little bit of happiness. And it was really irreconcilable for him, and this was all in his poetry.	TSO TSO TSO TSO TSO	TSO TSO TSO TSO TSO	Good support of pupil. Again, probing might give student a chance to develop this idea further.
S3: I was reading in our book that he wrote most of his poetry when he was dying of tuberculosis and that this affected his poetry—that this caused his negative capability—that he knew pretty soon he'd be dead.	SSO	SSR	Additional information initiated by student—would seem to indicate his interest in the topic.
T: Well, I don't know how you could ever prove it. This is in a lot of Russian literature, the problem of exactly what effect death has on an artist—the effect of his knowledge that he's going to die. But this is of course very hard to prove.	TSO TSO	TSO TSO	Good information introduced by teacher, but used more to shut off student rather than to support his inquiry.

LESSON	Coding		ANALYSIS
	Form I	Form II	
T: Okay, there is a poem that has very good examples of negative capability. Like I said, it is in just about everything he wrote. But there are excellent illustrations here. So I want you to read this poem (writing name on board) in your textbook and write a short paragraph. You can take either the poem as a whole, but I'll give you a hint, it's much easier to select short passages from the context of the poem. Negative capability is not a theme so much—this poem has a separate theme—but an element within a poem. Write a paragraph and tell me how what you selected illustrates negative capability. Then I'll collect them and we'll discuss negative capability some more.	TSO TSO TSO TSO TSO TSO TSO	TSO TSO TSO TSO TSO TSO TSO	At this point the teacher evidently feels the students are ready to read a poem and write about it from the viewpoint of the new concept that has been introduced. Those students who have participated in the discussion have provided evidence of this.

The paragraphs they write will provide the teacher with additional readiness information. |

DETERMINING READINESS: TEACHING EVALUATION AND FEEDBACK GUIDE*

TEACHER'S NAME _____ RATER'S NAME _____ DATE _____

EVALUATION CRITERIA	COMMENTS
1. Excellent. No real weakness. Most was determined. Relevant information was gained from all pupils.	
2. Good. At least one identifiable weakness. Much was determined.	
3. Acceptable. Enough was determined for lesson to be meaningful. Some important information was not gained.	
4. Serious weakness. Key aspects were not determined. Information vital to the success of the lesson was not gained.	
5. Vague attention to task. Many weaknesses. Little information was gained.	
6. No attention to task. No information was gained.	

BASIC TEACHING TASKS   circle one

I. Determining Readiness   1 2 3 4 5 6

*Read the sample lesson and evaluate it using this guide. Give a numerical rating and your comments. Compare your evaluation with those of your instructor and colleagues.

DETERMINING READINESS: SUGGESTED ACTIVITIES

1. If you are interested in exploring student attitudes toward your subject, one way to start your lesson is to invite students to talk about your subject area. What do they know about it? What relevant experiences have they had? In which aspects of the subject are they interested? Do they know why it is important to learn about the subject? What will knowledge of the subject enable them to do that they cannot do now?

2. Have a demonstration (by the instructor or a student) before the laboratory lesson on determining readiness. Demonstrations before each laboratory task will often serve to clarify the concepts involved in a task. Some demonstrations may utilize simulation of certain problems. For example, in determining readiness students can role-play various readiness problems encountered in a real classroom setting (a student who does not possess sufficient prior knowledge to profit from some lesson, one who does not see the purpose in learning about the content, a student who has mastered the material before the lesson is taught).

3. Information (and misinformation) about readiness can come from students' cumulative records on file in the school office. From sample cumulative records you might find out what types of information are typically kept and discuss what their value might be. For example, how might a student's grades and standardized achievement test scores in different subject areas help you plan for his instruction? How valid and how reliable are the different sources of information such as grades, standardized tests, and teacher comments?

4. Several films from the "Critical Moments in Teaching" series (Holt, Rinehart, and Winston) present realistic problems relevant to determining readiness. See especially "What Do I Know About Benny?", "Less Far than the Arrow," "Walls," and "Julia," for problems related to different aspects of readiness.

5. The focus of this lesson is obtaining information about one's students. However, you might turn things around and try to determine the kinds of information about yourself that you convey to your students. You will find the rating scales listed below useful for this purpose. After you have taught, you can ask observers, colleagues, and/or students to record their impressions using each scale. You might rate yourself on each scale so that you can compare your own perceptions with those of others. It is important that you have the opportunity to discuss these scales after their use to discover the basis for the ratings. Unless sufficient time is available to follow up this activity, we do not recommend it.

Check the space on each scale which describes the teacher's behavior.

warm   /___/___/___/___/___/___/ cold

quiet   /___/___/___/___/___/___/ out-going

confident   /___/___/___/___/___/___/ anxious

unfriendly   /___/___/___/___/___/___/ friendly

energetic   /___/___/___/___/___/___/ lethargic

concerned
with whether   /___/___/___/___/___/___/ doesn't care if I
I learn   learn

defensive   /___/___/___/___/___/___/ open

likes   /___/___/___/___/___/___/ dislikes
students   students

weak   /___/___/___/___/___/___/ forceful

unhappy   /___/___/___/___/___/___/ happy

thoughtless   /___/___/___/___/___/___/ considerate

interested   /___/___/___/___/___/___/ interested in
in my ideas   his own ideas

6. References:

For a provocative story of a youngster who was judged by his parents and teachers as mentally retarded, but who, under the understanding guidance of a counselor, turned out to be highly gifted and sensitive, read *Dibs: In Search of Self,* by Virginia M. Axline, New York: Ballantine Books, 1964.

For stimulating information and commentary on the concerns of adolescents in the United States, read *Coming of Age in America* by Edgar Z. Friedenberg, New York: Vingate Books, 1963.

For information on concerns of teachers, read *When Teachers Face Themselves,* by Arthur T. Jersild, New York: Teachers College Press, 1955; and "Concerns of Teachers: A Developmental Conceptualization" by Frances F. Fuller, *American Educational Research Journal,* March, 1969.

For detailed information on determining readiness in the areas of perceptual-motor skills, reading skills, written expression and spelling, speech and language disorders, arithmetic skills, and personal-emotional-social skills, read *Teacher Diagnosis of Educational Difficulties* by Robert M. Smith and others, Columbus, Ohio: Charles E. Merrill Books, Inc., 1969.

chapter 4

Clarifying Objectives

In your last lesson you gained information from your students relative to some topic or objective. You will, again, attempt to determine readiness for this lesson, but now a new task is added. This task challenges you to start thinking more precisely about what you are attempting to teach, that is, to clarify your learning objectives.

By clarifying objectives we mean communicating to your students what you want them to learn. This task can be viewed as consisting of three levels: (1) specifying the observable behavior (performance) which you intend; (2) detailing the conditions under which you expect the learning to be demonstrated; and (3) clarifying the meaning and acceptability of different levels of performance.

At the end of your lesson your students should be able to state, at a minimum, the type of observable behavior which is expected of them as a result of the lesson. For example, *to write a paragraph* using a topic sentence and several supporting sentences; or, *to give an oral summary* of two conflicting points of view regarding the role of the U.S. in aiding emergent nations and *to state their own opinion* on the issue; or, to hand in *a written English translation* of a set of French sentences whose verbs are in the future tense.

Beyond this minimum understanding of the lesson's objectives, you should try to make clear to the students both the conditions under which the attainment of the objective can be demonstrated and the level or range of acceptable performance. For instance, the student should be able to solve correctly a system of simultaneous equations (basic objective) in two unknowns (important condition) at least 70 percent of the time (acceptable level of performance); or, the student should be able to define photosynthesis (basic objective) using an illustration provided by the textbook (important condition) and using the terms oxygen, carbon dioxide, and clorophyll correctly in the definition (condition and performance criteria).

Clarifying objectives means communicating your expectations in terms of what pupils should be able to do as a result of your lesson. For example, suppose that you said, "Today we are going to learn about the history of the early colonial settlers." This does not give pupils a clear idea as to what is expected of them. They are "to learn"—but what does this mean? To be able to recall certain facts? To trace exploration routes? To write a summary?

The point is that for a teacher to clarify objectives, he must communicate to pupils what they will be expected to do when a sequence of instruction is completed. The infinitive "to do" signifies observable pupil behavior. When objectives are stated in such terms as "to learn," "to know," "to understand," and "to appreciate," no observable behavior is identified. Such objectives can be translated into behavioral objectives by using such words as "to recite," "to write," "to solve," and "to list."

Identifying observable behavior such as "to write," however, does not provide an entire solution to the problem of clarifying objectives. "To write a history of the early colonial settlers," for example, describes the behavior of writing, but the scope of the task is so broad that it gives little comfort to the pupil whose responsibility it is to interpret and act on the directions.

After a general type of behavior has been identified as the intended result of a lesson, the objective can be further clarified by three kinds of efforts. First, striving to describe the task in words with the fewest interpretations will help clarify your objectives. For example, "to write an interpretation of . . ." is more specific and consequently clearer than "to write a paper about . . . ." Such words as "translate," "interpret," "extrapolate," "analyze," "apply," "synthesize," and "evaluate" are relatively specific.

The second effort at clarification consists of stating the conditions under which the desired behavior is expected to occur. For example, how much time does the pupil have to attain the objective? What resources can he use? How many attempts will be allowed?

Third, and probably most difficult of all, stating levels of acceptable performance of the desired objectives will further clarify what is expected of pupils. For example, if a mathematics teacher has a computational skill as his objective, he may state his minimal level of performance as seven correct problems out of ten. However, if his objective consists of correct application of procedure, he will have to decide how many elements of the procedure must be mastered and in how many different ways it must be applied. Likewise, the social studies teacher will have to decide, for example, how many of the "given" facts must be included in the history summary, how many "new" facts must be introduced, and how much and what kind of interpretation will be minimally acceptable. In addition to specifying an acceptable level of performance, the teacher may elaborate on the meanings of several levels of performance. In other words, a really good job of clarifying objectives requires specifying characteristics of "A" performance, "B" performance, etc. In the cases where grades or some facsimile are not used, clarifying objectives requires communicating the criteria used to determine whether a student has learned certain content or can proceed to a new objective.

Thus far we have emphasized the clarification of the teacher's learning objectives. However, many teachers aspire to having the determination of learning objectives a joint enterprise between themselves and their students. A few teachers will want learning objectives for particular activities established entirely by students, possibly with each student setting his own objectives. The task of clarifying objectives is still relevant when students participate in the setting of objectives, but the farther you go in this direction, the more your task becomes one of helping students clarify their own objectives—as opposed to communicating your objectives. You can help them define their own objectives in terms of intended behavior, conditions, and performance criteria (but you need not take the fun out of it by using these terms).

Now that the purpose of clear objectives has been stressed, it is probably worthwhile to reflect on an important reality. Many experienced teachers recognize that teaching and learning can and do take place without the continual clarification by the teacher of every objective. Those teachers who have conscientiously attempted to translate general goals into behaviorally oriented statements of objectives know that this is an extremely difficult, and at times seemingly impossible, task. The point is, however, that if you do not have a clear behavioral notion as to what you are after, difficult as it may be to formulate, then you cannot clearly communicate your goals to your students. Furthermore, you will have difficulty designing appropriate learning strategies, and your pupils will be unclear about where they have been and where they are going. In short, you may indeed be teaching, but you will not be certain what you are trying to teach, how best to teach it, how to determine if you have succeeded, or even whether it is worth the effort to try.

The task of "clarifying objectives" should be "clarified" by the levels of performance indicated on the Evaluation and Feedback Guide on page 49. You should use this guide in evaluating the sample lesson on page 55. You may also find it useful to go back to the written lesson for determining readiness to reevaluate it in terms of how clear the objectives were.

STRATEGIES FOR CLARIFYING OBJECTIVES

The kinds of strategies you use to clarify objectives will depend to a great extent on the kind of lesson you are teaching. If your lesson is attitude oriented, your objectives may be revealed late in the lesson or possibly after the lesson is over. Also, some objectives contain concepts whose meaning would not be clear until after some explanation, so a complete statement of an objective might not occur until later in instruction. For other lessons, the sooner you can clarify the objectives, the more appropriate it will be. When you are working to help pupils clarify their objectives, still other strategies may be called for.

Each of the following strategies for clarifying objectives will be appropriate for some lessons and inappropriate for others. You should select those strategies which seem best suited for communicating your objectives.

Stating the Objectives of a Lesson

One of the most obvious ways of clarifying your objectives for students is simply to tell them what is expected. This may be done orally or possibly in writing. It may be done at the beginning, during, and/or at the end of a lesson. Such explanations should be behaviorally stated, contain a specific description of the task, and contain descriptions of the desired conditions and levels of performance. This statement can take the form, "By the end of the lesson, you should be able to do something (describe it), under certain conditions (name them), with a certain degree (specify) of proficiency." For example, "After we have practiced the use of the hyphen, colon, and semicolon on the typewriter keyboard, you should be able to type a 300-word letter from a copy, having ten of these punctuation marks, and make no more than one error on these ten marks;" or "Today we are going to discuss characterization, so after our discussion you should be able to tell what this means, in your own words. Then I will ask you to read a story and describe at least one example of characterization in it."

Although you may have sufficiently clarified your objectives in your own mind, and your statement of these to your pupils may be accurate, this does not ensure adequate communication of the objectives to your pupils. The objectives may be stated so quickly that students cannot comprehend what is being said. Or possibly the objectives are so complex that even though they were initially understood, after a few minutes students cannot recall them. Possibly students can restate the objectives but do not understand them in terms of being able "to do," that is, the students lack behavioral referents for the words you used. For example, students may be able to say "to be able to circumscribe a rectangle" yet have no idea what "to circumscribe" means.

Examples of Expected Performance

Using examples of desired behavior is a useful strategy for clarifying objectives. An example might be presented by a finished sketch, a written paragraph, or a demonstration. Or you might ask students to present an example as an indication of their comprehension. You might also teach students to accomplish a part of the objective, to increase their comprehension of the whole objective. For instance, to have students understand that "the generation gap" results partially from a lack of meaningful communication may help clarify the objective, "To describe at least one reason why lack of contact can sometimes result in conflict between groups of people." The use of examples, which are meaningful to your students—within their frames of reference—should greatly enhance pupil comprehension of your objectives.

Clarity of Presentation

A well organized lesson should add to the degree to which your objectives are communicated to your students. The different parts of your lesson should be

CLARIFYING OBJECTIVES: EVALUATION AND FEEDBACK GUIDE

CRITERIA	COMMENTS
II. Clarifying Objectives	

II. Clarifying Objectives

1. Excellent. All aspects were clear. I can accurately explain the objectives of the lesson. I know what behavior is expected of me. I understand the conditions under which the behavior is expected. I understand how well I am supposed to do or at least what different levels of performance mean.

2. Good. Most was clear. I can accurately explain most of what is expected of me. Some aspect of conditions or levels of performance is not entirely clear to me.

3. Acceptable. Enough was clear that I could learn from the lesson. Although several aspects of the desired behaviors are not clear to me, I gained enough to begin the lesson or assignment. I anticipate that in the context of the lesson, the objectives will become clear.

4. Serious weakness. Much was not clear. Although I had a vague notion about what was expected, I could not describe the desired behavior. I feel uneasy about starting the lesson.

5. Vague attention to task. Many weaknesses. Most was not clear. The lesson contained contradictory statements of desired behavior. No examples were given which helped to clarify. I feel confused and unprepared to begin the lesson.

6. No attention to task. Total confusion. There appeared to be no attention to the clarification of objectives. I have no idea what is expected of me.

I. Determining Readiness   1 2 3 4 5 6
II. Clarifying Objectives   1 2 3 4 5 6

arranged to facilitate communication of the objectives. For example, it may be appropriate for pupils to be engaged in an activity, but only after the purpose of the activity has been explained. Secondly, each part of your lesson should relate to the objectives of the lesson. If part of the lesson is "off the track" or inconsistent with the stated objectives, this will lead to confusion about what is really intended. For example, a teacher may say that the objective of a lesson is the interpretation of a poem, while the content of the lesson involves a discussion of the author's life. Unless the relationship between the author's life and interpreting the poem are made clear, students may infer from the lesson that they are supposed to know certain facts about the author's life.

The way you communicate in general will be related to your ability to communicate learning objectives. Thus general skills of good communication are relevant here as well as in all of your subsequent lessons. You should attend to your eye contact with your pupils, your speech habits, including your ability to speak audibly and clearly, your use of inflection for appropriate emphases, and a moderate rate of speech (going too fast or too slowly will be problems for some).

Use of Questions

Asking questions to determine whether objectives have been communicated is certainly a relevant clarification strategy. Early in your lesson you may start to seek feedback. A question such as "Do you understand what we are going to learn?" may be useful when a student senses a specific problem and has the courage to speak up, but generally a question which necessitates a demonstration of comprehension will be more useful. For example, you might ask a pupil for an example, a restatement, or an elaboration of the objective.

Summarizing

Near the end of your lesson you may need to tie elements of the lesson together to enhance communication of your objectives. You may give the summary or you may draw it from your pupils. While the summary may be preplanned, it should account for unanticipated aspects of the lesson. For example, you may have been "side-tracked" for several minutes of your lesson, and you will want to emphasize if possible its relationship to the main objectives of the lesson. Although the summary may be a simple repetition of the objectives of the lesson, it may serve to reveal the objectives for the first time or it may be a revised statement of objectives, depending on what happened during the lesson.

In deciding which strategy or strategies to use in this lesson, you should attend to the criterion: Do the students understand the objectives of the lesson? It is much more appropriate to select one or two strategies to communicate the objectives clearly than to try all the strategies and create confusion. Your choice of a strategy will represent a hypothesis: students will know what they are to accomplish as a result of this lesson if these behaviors are employed. The feedback you receive about the lesson will provide information, and that should help you make future decisions about how to clarify instructional objectives.

OBSERVATION FORM

The observation form which follows may be used in two ways. First, a colleague or instructor can observe your lesson, classifying statements and questions into the appropriate categories. You will then have an objective description of behavior during the lesson. The second use of the observation form is for self-analysis. That is, if your lesson has been tape recorded (audio or video), you may listen to or view it and record your own and your students' verbal behavior.

This observation form is intended to provide feedback about the behaviors used to clarify objectives and student response to the lesson. Use of the form is relatively simple: every five seconds the observer must decide which category best describes the content of that five seconds.[1] Then a check mark is placed in the row corresponding to that category. Verbal behavior is first divided into teacher categories or student categories, then into statements (provides information) or questions (solicits information). Finally, the statements or questions are coded according to whether they deal with the objective's intended behavior, conditions, or performance criterion, or with other information.

For example, if a student asks, "How many new words are we supposed to translate?" a tally would be made for *"Student* behavior, *solicits* information regarding *performance criteria."* Probably the teacher's answer would be coded as *"Teacher* behavior, *provides* information regarding *performance criteria."*

The basic information available in this form can answer the following questions about the lesson's objectives:

1. How much time was spent by the teacher clarifying objectives?
2. What kinds of information were provided?
3. How much information about objectives was solicited by the teacher and by the students?
4. What kinds of information were solicited?

Other kinds of information which may or may not be relevant to the objectives are also available: e.g., relative amounts of teacher- and student-talk and relative amounts of teacher and student behavior not related to the objective.

Examples of the various categories used in this form can be found by referring to the second column of the sample lesson where the behaviors in the lesson are coded.

---

[1]If a statement or question lasts less than five seconds, code whatever behavior occupies the largest part of the five seconds. Do not code silence.

OBSERVATION FORM* FOR CLARIFYING OBJECTIVES

CATEGORIES			CODE	TALLIES
Teacher Behavior	*Provides* information about objectives regarding	Intended behavior	TPI	
		Conditions	TPC	
		Performance criteria	TPP	
	Teacher provides other information not related to objectives		TPO	
	Solicits information about objectives regarding	Intended behavior	TSI	
		Conditions	TSC	
		Performance criteria	TSP	
	Teacher solicits other information not related to objectives		TSO	
Student Behavior	*Provides* information about objectives regarding	Intended behavior	SPI	
		Conditions	SPC	
		Performance criteria	SPP	
	Student provides other information not related to objectives		SPO	
	Solicits information about objectives regarding	Intended behavior	SSI	
		Conditions	SSC	
		Performance criteria	SSP	
	Student solicits other information not related to objectives		SSO	

*Reliable use of this form will require approximately two hours of practice. If the three categories pertaining to objectives (behavior, conditions, criteria) are combined into one overall category, the system will be learned much more readily. Of course, no information will be available then about distinctions among these three aspects of objectives.

CLARIFYING OBJECTIVES:
LESSON FOR ANALYSIS AND EVALUATION

LESSON	CODE	ANALYSIS
T: I have two pictures here I want you to look at carefully and think about. Just look at them for a few seconds. Barbara and Bill, move in here close so you can see. (Teacher places two mounted pictures on the board chalk tray; one is of the five marines raising the flag over Iwo Jima; the other shows several badly wounded soldiers riding a troop carrier.) (Pause 5 seconds)	TPO	Dramatic material selected to provoke involvement.
S: What are we supposed to be looking for?	SSI	Pupil apparently feels the need to have the purpose of this activity clarified.
T: Just look at them carefully and think about what you see. (Pause 15 seconds)	TPO	
T: Now who would like to tell me what they see in these two pictures? Tell me anything you want to about these pictures—anything you think, anything you feel, Susan.	TSO	Teacher repeats directions but keeps the task quite open and vague—at least initially the discussion will depend upon the students' interpretations. The objective seems to involve a discussion.
S1: Well, that one seems to be showing us the good side of war—glory and all that. And that one shows the bad side—blood and suffering, misery, maybe a waste of human life.	SPO SPO	
T: All right. Bill?		Rather than pursuing the first comment teacher chooses to elicit additional reactions.
S2: Really, they're just different pictures of war. But the one is kind of the way we think of Vietnam and the other is how we think of America's past wars—especially World War II.	SPO SPO	
T: Good observation. These pictures do come from the two wars you mention. Ted, how about you? What do you see?	TSO	Further solicitation. New student brought in.
S3: I think mostly of that one picture—of Vietnam and what we're in over there. Too bad we couldn't just raise up a flag like that and be done with it.	SPO	
T: Would you go to help raise the flag—I mean our flag and the South Vietnamese flag—to help gain the victory? Carl?	TSO	For the first time teacher directs the discussion by raising this question. New student brought into discussion.

LESSON	CODE	ANALYSIS
S4: I was mostly thinking about the terrible struggle it took to get the flag up in that picture—there were probably hundreds of pictures like that one—but yes I will go. When the time comes, if the war is still dragging on, of course I'll go.	SPO SPO	
T: Susan, what about that?	TSO	Teacher invites a student to respond to another student—
S1: All I can see is the confusion and the waste. Personally I don't want to be a part of that mess—at least I would not want my father or husband or brother to have to go. Maybe this is selfish, but to me my life is more important than fighting in a stupid war.	SPO SPO	opens up student-to-student interaction. Conflict was created by calling on Susan.
S3: That's really silly.	SPO	
S1: Well, it's my life.		
S3 and S4: (exasperated) What?		
S4: What if we all felt that way? Boy would we be in bad shape—that's really a selfish point of view.	SPO	
S1: Well what are we fighting for in Vietnam anyway—that you're so excited about getting killed about?	SPO SSO	
T: Wait. Wait. Susan, Bill, calm down. Listen to others for a minute. Let's see what some of the rest of you think. Cathy, how about you?	TSO	Some information given here on the kind of discussion behavior desired. Teacher reexerts control of the discussion and chooses to bring additional students into the discussion. Up to this point a spirited discussion has been provoked but little information has been given on the objectives of the lesson.
S5: Well, I agree with Bill. I think these are important things we're fighting for in Vietnam, and when your country's in a war you have to fight.	SPO	
T: And Barbara, what do you think?	TSO	
S6: I agree with Cathy.	SPO	
T: What do you mean you agree with Cathy?	TSO	
S6: Well, I think when your country's fighting you have to fight.	SPO	
T: What about Susan's point? Don't you think you have to think about how many lives might be involved?	TSO	

LESSON	CODE	ANALYSIS
S6: Well, I suppose you do.	SPO	
S3: What would we be today if people hadn't given their lives for our country?	SSO	
S4: Well, what does that mean? Your country is your country . . .	SSO SPO	
T: Okay, okay. Let's think for a few minutes. I was hoping the pictures would get you thinking about war and the meanings of war and how you personally react to war, and they really seem to have done that, especially for a couple of you. The questions you raised are really important ones. You have to try to answer them together—trying not to fly off the handle too quickly. Now I want you to keep the same enthusiasm and concern but to look at the problem of going to war from a different perspective. You have read Chapter Five for background on America's fight for Independence from Britain.	TPI TPI TPO TPC TPC	Purpose of the discussion is now stated. Desired discussion behavior is elaborated.
Now I'll ask you to read these two handouts (I'll pass them out in a minute) which describe two colonists. One of them decided to go to war with the revolutionaries. The other decided to support the Mother Country. Now, what I want you to try to decide is what you would have done had you been a colonist —would you fight for or against the revolutionaries—or would you fight at all?	TPC TPO TPI	The primary objective of the lesson is now introduced. The assigned reading materials are conditions, that is, preferred input, to the papers.
I want you to write down your decision and in one or two pages tell why you chose the way you did. Give at least three good reasons for your decisions. You should turn these in tomorrow, and we'll discuss them and also come back to talking about Vietnam. Is the assignment clear now? What are you supposed to do? Barbara would you summarize the assignment for us?	TPI TPP TPC TSI	Acceptable level of performance is suggested. What is a "good" reason? Teacher questions student—seeks feedback on how well the assignment was communicated.
S6: Well, we're supposed to tell why we'd fight in the Revolutionary War—I mean who'd we fight for.	SPI	

T: Okay, good. And what material should you use? Carl?	TSC	Additional feedback sought. This is serving to reinforce the initial directions.
S4: The chapter from the book and the material you're going to give us.	SPC	
S1: Are these going to be graded?	SSP	Student seeks information on levels of performance.
T: They'll be graded satisfactory if you give three reasons which are well thought out and if not, I'll ask you to work on them some more.	TPP	Teacher elaborates the acceptable level of performance and clarifies it in terms of "grades."
S2: What if we can't decide what to do?	SSI	
T: Then do the best you can to give the reasons for not being able to decide—but the war is coming and if you're not with the revolutionaries then you're probably against them.	TPI	Student seeks further information on intended behavior.
Okay, let me go over the assignment once more. Make sure you have read the chapter on the American Revolution, that's pages 68 to 89, and the two handouts, and then write how and why you would choose sides if you were a colonist at that time. Just like you were starting to defend your ideas on Vietnam, try to defend your decision on the Revolutionary War. Remember to try to give at least three reasons for your position. Any other questions?	TPI TPC TPI TPI TPP	Objective is restated. Teacher uses example from discussion to clarify the objective.

CLARIFYING OBJECTIVES: SUGGESTED ACTIVITIES

1. Write a lesson plan in which you specify your lesson objectives in terms of intended behavior. Describe the conditions and acceptable levels of performance.

2. Present your lesson to a colleague prior to teaching it in the lab. Pay particular attention to how you handle unanticipated questions and responses.

3. After your laboratory lesson, have each student write down his understanding of your objectives. Compare these statements to each other and to your written statement of objectives.

4. View the film "Walls" from Holt, Rinehart and Winston's series, *Critical Moments in Teaching* for an interesting problem in both determining readiness and communicating objectives.

5. As an exercise in determining how well people listen, divide into groups of three. Two students should serve as "discussants" and one as an observer-recorder. Alternate the roles. The discussants should pursue some topic of mutual interest, such as "What major goals are of most importance for U.S. public schools?" The observer should, from time to time, halt the discussion to ask each person what the other has been saying. The observer and the speaker should feed back how accurately the third person has restated a position.

6. References:

For an unusually clear and uniquely presented explanation of how to clarify your teaching objectives, read *Preparing Objectives for Programmed Instruction* by Robert F. Mager, San Francisco: Fearon Publishers, 1962.

Helpful guidance on asking questions appropriate to different kinds of teaching objectives can be found in *Classroom Questions: What Kinds?* by Norris M. Sanders, New York: Harper & Row, 1966.

Considerable information on trends in secondary education in general and specific subject fields can be found in *Secondary Education: A Textbook of Readings* by John J. Deboer, Walter Kaulfers, and Lawrence E. Metcalf, Boston: Allyn and Bacon, Inc., 1966. Information on these trends may give you ideas about the types of teaching objectives which you consider most appropriate.

chapter 5

Motivating

By this time in the laboratory, you have probably received enough feedback that you are beginning to formulate relatively new thoughts about yourself as a teacher. You may be questioning your own readiness for being a teacher. You may be questioning the clarity of your reasons for wanting to be a teacher. And, relative to the task for this chapter, you may be questioning your motivation for being a teacher.

Many laboratory teachers (particularly preservice teachers) begin to raise these highly personal and important questions at this point in the laboratory. By now, some teachers are beginning to develop conceptions of and motivations for teaching which were previously unrealized; that is, some teachers are really starting to get excited about being a teacher. Other lab teachers are beginning to have serious doubts about teaching, even though their performances in the lab may have been quite successful. These teachers are gaining firsthand experience and intense feedback, and they are finding that these experiences are not satisfying their needs or providing the kinds of challenges they are looking for.

Many teachers at this point in the laboratory experience are between these extremes but have felt some degree of frustration. Things aren't going as well as they would like, and they feel frustrated that they aren't achieving the kind of successes they feel are possible.

Although we hope that each lab lesson provides experience and information for continuing improvement of your ability to teach, we find that for many teachers the motivating lab is a turning point in terms of their frustration. For example, one lab teacher wrote in his diary:

Before the lab: I am very concerned about this lab because I have not yet had even one satisfying teaching experience in the lab. Thank goodness for the listening ear of my wife in which I poured all my doubts about my capability to make someone interested enough in what I was saying to listen—and learn. After talking around everything and brooding, out loud, over my inability to teach a good lesson, I simply asked myself what I would think was an intelligent, probing thing for a person to teach about—that is, what would I really like to express to a group (if I were not thinking of myself as "the teacher"). I have decided I will simply deal with happiness. I will ask each person what makes them happy and why. To create interaction and knowledge of another person, as well as self-knowledge, I will ask each person to express what his opinion of another person's answer is. If I become genuinely involved in the discussion, I think it will interest the students.

After the lab: For the first time I am satisfied with a lesson. I learned not only how I could improve my lessons and my interaction with people, but I learned something about the very people I was talking with. I really enjoyed the lesson—was sorry I had to stop.

Another teacher (physical education), prior to the motivation lesson, had taught three lessons in which she attempted to impart knowledge about exercising (first lesson), volleyball (second lesson), and badminton (third lesson). She was feeling very frustrated with the lack of response she was getting from her pupils, and if previous lessons were any indication, her motivation lesson was going to be her first real failure. Realizing this, she decided to take a different approach to her field. She decided she would have to be a less important focus of the lesson, and would have to get her students into the act and involved in the lesson. Her lesson involved learning a folk dance, and she immediately engaged her students in attempting to perform the dance to the rhythm of accompanying music. The teacher was exhilarated with her lesson—especially when students later left the laboratory skipping along with their new dance steps. "Why didn't I get them involved in my first lesson?" she asked in her lesson evaluation. And later in the lab experience, she reflected back:

It was during the dance lesson that I made a real breakthrough. Suddenly I realized I was really helping students learn something, and I was having fun doing it. And then when I realized they were also having fun—well, I just felt great.

Whether or not this lab lesson provides a breakthrough for you, it should present a significant challenge. Of all the dimensions of teaching that are important, and of all the concerns that teachers have, motivating students to learn is probably the most important.

MOTIVATING: OBJECTIVE

The task of motivating involves the problem of creating interest in your lesson, particularly in achieving the objectives of your lesson. The use of student "interest" in this context should be extended to include persistence and effort to attain learning objectives.

Motivating will be considered as comprising two levels: the first level consists of gaining student attention; the second level goes a step farther and demands that students willingly participate in the lesson. These two levels may be treated as two separate lab lessons, that is, in the first lesson strategies for gaining attention will be used; for the second lesson, strategies for gaining participation will be employed. Or, both kinds of motivating objectives and strategies may be combined in one lesson.

The following evaluation and feedback guide describes six states of motivation. The highest two states of motivation can be viewed as reflecting "participation" in a lesson. The next four states describe varying degrees of "attention" to a lesson. Note that the first two basic teaching tasks are also included at the bottom of the guide, since clarifying objectives and determining readiness should also be attended to during this lesson.

MOTIVATING STRATEGIES

Before proceeding to specific motivating strategies we should reflect on the relevance of the two previous tasks to this dimension of teaching. Giving students a chance to provide information about themselves (determining readiness) may in and of itself have a motivational effect because it indicates that the teacher is interested in the students.

To select objectives in terms of pupil readiness is crucial to motivation. Your students' knowledge and abilities relative to a particular objective will have a significant impact on their motivation to achieve that objective. For example, should many of your students lack an understanding of some concept necessary for accomplishing the objective of your lesson, and subsequently fail to learn anything, their interest in pursuing the lesson will probably be low. On the other hand, if you determine this lack of understanding and provide instruction to make up for it, then your chance of maintaining student interest is considerably enhanced.

Effective clarification of objectives will also enhance interest in your lesson. Although clear objectives are not of themselves necessarily motivating, they provide a condition for appropriate motivation. That is, they clarify what is expected of the student and focus his attention on what is important, rather than leave him in a state of confusion about what is expected, or perhaps in a state of undirected interest. Clear objectives relevant to students' felt needs and within students' abilities to achieve will certainly provide conditions for a high rate of interest on the part of students.

Brief descriptions of motivating strategies are presented below. If the task of motivating is divided into two lessons, you should choose from the first set (strategies for gaining attention) for the first lesson, and from the second set (strategies for gaining participation) for the second lesson. Whatever strategies you choose, you should realize that no strategy or combination of strategies will ever guarantee effective classroom motivation. Motivation will be a continuous

MOTIVATING: TEACHING EVALUATION AND FEEDBACK GUIDE

TEACHER'S NAME _____ RATER'S NAME _____ DATE _____

EVALUATION CRITERIA	RATER'S COMMENTS
III. Motivating	

1. Excellent. Extremely interested. I enjoyed the lesson very much. I wanted to continue with the lesson. I would like to know more about the topic, to the extent that I would seek information on my own. (Pupils initiate responses; e.g., ask many questions, suggest activities.)

2. Good. Interested. I enjoyed the lesson. I would like to learn more about the topic, but probably wouldn't seek extra information, or work beyond what was required. (Pupils respond to the lesson appropriately; e.g., answer questions enthusiastically, engage in relevant activities.)

3. Acceptable. Somewhat interested. Most aspects of the lesson interested me. I might like to explore this topic further, but not right away. (Pupils attend to the lesson; e.g., maintain eye contact, take notes.)

4. Serious weakness. Somewhat uninterested. Some aspects of the lesson were interesting. I would be very unlikely to pursue this topic further on my own. (Some inattentiveness displayed; e.g., looking out of the window.)

5. Vague attention to task. Uninterested. Virtually no aspect of this lesson interested me. I have little, if any, desire to know more about this topic. (Much inattentiveness displayed.)

6. No attention to task. Very uninterested. I was very bored. I have lost whatever interest I once had in this topic; enthusiasm I did show was squelched. (Pupils ignored lesson; engaged in unrelated activities.)

BASIC TEACHING TASKS

I. Determining Readiness   1 2 3 4 5 6
II. Clarifying Objectives   1 2 3 4 5 6
III. Motivating   1 2 3 4 5 6

challenge relative to your own changing interests and abilities, to particular lesson objectives, and to the readiness of your pupils.

Strategies for Gaining Attention

1. Communicating rationale for objectives

This strategy consists of making clear to students the importance of and reasons for attaining an objective. You can approach this strategy in two ways.

a. By stating the immediate and/or long range consequences of attaining the objective. For example, "By learning these spelling rules, you will do much better on your spelling tests, and when you write paragraphs you won't have to spend as much time looking up words in the dictionary to find out how to spell them." "When you have learned to identify charged words, you will be able to identify an author's bias more readily. You will also be able to influence other people's viewpoint more readily in your own writing." "You should learn how to solve this type of equation, because when you get to the next chapter, the new material assumes that you know how. Also, if you can solve these equations, you will be able to figure out more story problems. Incidentally, we will see how these equations help figure out how to measure and construct cabinets and furniture."

b. Another procedure for communicating a rationale is to solicit student ideas. Students are often able to state reasons for pursuing some objective, and these reasons may be just as important, or more important, than those stated by the teacher. A simple question such as "John, what reasons do you see for learning how to . . . ?" is an excellent way to begin a discussion of objectives. This procedure is particularly appropriate before embarking on a long unit, since it will provide readiness information that you may later use to determine projects and assignments.

2. Arousing curiosity

New or unexplained phenomena will arouse the curiosity of many students. You may present content (information, concepts, ideas) from your field which is new to your students. You may find that unanswered questions, unsolved problems, or unexplained phenomena (e.g., a poster, quotation, or chemical reaction) will arouse students' curiosity.

A different, unexpected, or personalized approach to your content may serve to stimulate pupil interest. For example, the feudal system is traditionally presented by means of a graphic display of levels and functions. Approaching the feudal system from the point of view of a participant may be unexpected and personalized. The mention of poetry raises a myriad of stereotypes, often negative, in the minds of many pupils; one English teacher's unique introduction to poetry consisted of having his pupils consider why one person writes poetry and another one (most of the pupils included) does not.

Also useful for arousing curiosity are questions or problems that present some altered consequence to students. For instance, what would happen if the world stopped rotating on its axis? If no one had a thumb, would our lives be any different? If people could write only in the same style they talked, would books be easier or harder to read?

3. Creating dissonance or shock

This strategy is related to those suggested for arousing curiosity, the difference being a matter of degree. While the former entice the learner to attend, this strategy is designed to propel or demand the attention of the learner. For example, while a curiosity arousing strategy might be a presentation of a value conflict in our society, a shock strategy would be to get a student to recognize a glaring inconsistency in his own values. The chemical reaction of the arousing curiosity strategy may involve an emittance of bubbles; the shock reaction will be an explosion. Staging an experience is one way that teachers create an appropriate shock stimulus. For example, a teacher who wanted to have his students determine how accurately they could observe asked a student to rush into the room shouting and behaving in predetermined ways and then to exit quickly. The students then listed what they had seen and heard, and compared their perceptions to the actual event. Another teacher who wanted to have students consider human reactions to hysteria, staged a wild outbreak of emotionalism between panel members who were supposed to discuss the pros and cons of a particular issue.

4. Altering the physical learning environment

Too often we accept the given arrangement of the classroom without regard to our learning objectives. Classroom seating arrangements should be arranged to facilitate the kind of interaction desired. For example, a circle of chairs will greatly enhance equal communication between all participants in a discussion, and groups of chairs facing one another directly will add to group cohesion and sharpen exchanges in a debate. Just rearranging the seating pattern will create interest based on the change itself. Remember, you don't accept the seating pattern because that's the way you found it—organize your students according to your own objectives.

Many other aspects of the physical learning environment may be altered. Maps, objects, books, pictures, charts, overhead projectors, films, film strips, and other learning aids can be used to make the classroom more interesting as well as to increase interest in your objectives. While too many stimuli could result in confusion, the classroom is too often at the other extreme, drab and barren of exciting stimuli.

Another approach to varying the classroom environment is to go beyond the usual classroom setting. Libraries, museums, factories, even the shade of a tree provide different environments which may both stimulate interest and be appropriate to your learning objectives.

5. Shifting patterns of instruction

Any single mode of instruction, if maintained over certain periods of time, will probably reduce pupil attention. Even in a short lesson, you may find that varying your approach by including a presentation, an activity, or a discussion will increase attention.

6. Shifting sensory channels

Too often we think only of listening and looking (usually reading) as the ways to go about learning. The attention-producing idea offered here is that you consider using several sensory channels within your lesson. Through verbal directions you can guide pupils to attend to an object by *looking, touching, tasting,* and/or *smelling.* You can focus attention on something said by directing pupils to *listen.* Part of your lesson may require listening, while another part requires looking, and still another part requires manipulation of an object. You can aid pupils in shifting sensory channels by verbally emphasizing the desired channel and by reducing the extent to which other channels can be used to gain the desired information. For example, if students are to generalize about the texture of pieces of material, emphasize that they *look at* and *touch* the material before they talk about it. An English lesson about the effects of communication could include students drawing the image a paragraph or story conveys.

7. Using movement

The strategy suggested here is that you conduct yourself within the teaching space in such a way that your movements draw attention to desired phenomena. As a beginning, if you find yourself remaining stationary behind a desk, consider moving to some other part of the classroom. Movement to the left or right side of the classroom could be used to draw attention to a map or to a point written on the blackboard. Movement to the back of the classroom could be used to allow attention to focus on a pupil who is at the front of the room or to draw attention to pupils who are speaking in the back of the room. Moving near or among students should serve to raise the attention of those pupils nearest to you.

8. Using gestures and voice inflection

Just as bodily movement within the teaching space can create variety and draw attention to desired phenomena, movement of one's head and hands as well as facial expressions and voice inflection can gain attention in desired ways. Appropriate gestures and voice inflections will enhance the effectiveness of your presentations when used to emphasize those parts of the presentation which you consider most important. These often subtle behaviors can also enhance your ability to communicate generally by aiding the effectiveness of such behaviors as probing, positively reinforcing, redirecting interaction, and showing pleasure, doubt, thoughtfulness, etc.

9. Avoiding distracting behaviors

Just as some types of behavior serve to focus student attention on learning objectives, other behaviors serve to distract or focus attention away from a lesson. For example, the overuse of "uh," pacing, or the tapping of a pencil would usually distract attention from a lesson. Looking away from students and turning your back to the class are common behaviors which also create interference.

Strategies for Gaining Participation

One of the key elements involved in gaining participation from students in learning activities, is the necessity of individualizing instruction, that is, to make your instruction appropriate to the "state of readiness" of each individual pupil. This is of course an extremely difficult task, particularly when you are responsible for the instruction of large groups of students; nevertheless, attention to individualization and the use of flexible strategies should help you achieve acceptable levels of individualization. To effectively use the following strategies you will need to make appropriate use of your knowledge concerning the individual differences of your students.

1. Questioning

Questions, by definition, intend responses (or participation). Skilled questioning includes the ability to ask the appropriate question of a class or a particular individual. The appropriate question will require effort, yet will offer the respondent a fair chance for a successful answer.

Divergent questions, that is, questions which have more than one appropriate answer, are excellent for achieving participation. When these questions solicit opinions of some issue or topic, every student has a chance to contribute to a discussion.

Extending or probing questions also encourage participation. These questions ask students to give reasons for their opinions, or draw implications and applications. Some general types of extending questions are: "Do you *agree* with that statement (or opinion)?" "*Why* do you think that would be the case?" "What would be a *consequence* (Implication, inference) of that?" "How does that make you *feel?*"

2. Positive reinforcement

Postive reinforcement of a response will usually increase the probability that it will be repeated. Thus positive reinforcement of desired types of pupil behavior should result in more of that behavior. Attention to the following three types of reinforcement may help you use reinforcing strategies which increase pupil participation:

a. Simple verbal: Teacher statements which praise or encourage pupil behavior. Examples: "Very good," "Go on, you're on the right track," "That was well done."

    b. Complex verbal: Teacher statements which, in addition to praising or encouraging pupil behavior, give the reason for the praise. Examples: "Very good; you identified all the correct answers." "Excellent; you saw an economic principle underlying both depressions."

    c. Nonverbal: Gestures or facial expressions which communicate praise or encouragement. These may accompany or be independent of verbal reinforcement. Examples: smiling, nodding in agreement, touching (a pat on the back).

These reinforcers, rather than being used after each desired pupil response, will usually be intimately bound up in the interaction between the teacher and students. For example, building upon and using student ideas may function as a kind of complex verbal reinforcement. These are teacher statements which incorporate the ideas of students and are usually used in conjunction with extending questions. A basic skill involved in this strategy is the ability to summarize accurately the previous contributions of students and then ask an extending question based on the summary. For example: "John has pointed out that the proportion of electoral college votes for the winning candidate has not been equivalent to his share of the popular vote, and I think he has said that he feels this is unfair, but Sally has said that minority groups would have less influence if our elections were decided on the basis of only popular vote. Then are there other factors besides popular vote that you feel should be taken into consideration in choosing a president?"

A contrast to the previous kind of positive reinforcement is the teacher who says, "All right, this is a very interesting discussion, but the point *I* wanted to make is . . ."

Two points are important in use of praise and encouragement. First, praise is not always reinforcing. When a phrase is used so habitually ("Good, good.") that it becomes a speech habit, its potency as a reinforcer is reduced. Or if praise is given only to "good" pupils, it may become a negative reinforcer, and students may behave so as to avoid it. The second point is that it is very important to pay attention to *what* you are reinforcing. If you are attempting to get students to give reasons for their opinions, then you should reinforce student statements of reasons and not just the statement of the opinions alone.

Effective reinforcement requires using a variety of reinforcers in appropriate and sincere ways. We are not encouraging you to attempt to contrive reinforcements for every desired pupil response. But often when teachers first view themselves on videotape, they say: "I didn't realize I showed so little support of my pupils' responses." The challenge is to learn to express more fully your real excitement for your pupils' learning.

3. Feedback

Knowledge of results, or feedback, is an important strategy not only for motivation, but also learning. *Effective feedback* requires that you provide information to your students about their progress toward some objective, so that the students eventually acquire the ability to monitor their own performance. Important conditions which you can provide the student prior to feedback are:

    a. A clear understanding of the objective, including the satisfactory performance criteria.

    b. A description of the steps or sequence of behaviors that the student can follow to attain the objective.

Feedback will then consist of describing the extent to which the student has succeeded in accomplishing the objectives and helping the student discover which steps need additional work.

When you use feedback as a strategy in the lab or classroom, you need to do more than comment on the student's performance. You should be certain that the objectives and the steps necessary for attaining them are clear to the student. Once this condition is met, the student will be more able to use information about his performance.

There are three common types of feedback:

    a. Verbal confirmation: Teacher agrees with student: "That's right," "O.K.," "Yes." Used when it is clear that the student understands his response and needs no further elaboration.

    b. Verbal description: Teacher indicates agreement or disagreement and states why. "Your solution was correct for most cases, but you should also consider . . ." "You left out these two steps which are needed to complete the assignment correctly."

    c. Written description: Combined with positive reinforcers ("Very good paper! A. Excellent") and negative reinforcers ("Ugh, F"), written feedback informs the student of his areas of strength and weakness relative to a particular objective. Thus, your written feedback to students will be most helpful to them when you specify what aspects of their performance were outstanding and which were not, and how to improve deficiencies. The comment "Interesting paper, B" may be postively reinforcing for some students (but not A students); however, it does not supply information about what is interesting, nor how to improve on the performance.

4. Increasing expectation of success

This strategy might be most usefully applied to those students whose past performance has given them a little indication that their future efforts will be rewarded with success. We have all heard students (even successful college students) express a feeling of fear over taking some subject, because they feel they won't be able to understand it.

The basic tasks required of the teacher are:

    a. Short range objectives which are clear and can be readily accomplished.
    b. Frequent reinforcement for achievement and effortful behavior.
    c. Gradual introduction of longer range and more difficult objectives.

In the lab you may wish to try this strategy with a group of colleagues who have had difficulty with some subject you will teach. A good application of this strategy would be to define very specific and easily attainable objectives, give students the opportunity to accomplish these during the lesson, and provide them feedback about their results, along with reinforcement.

5. Role-playing

Role-playing is an activity in which the players (i.e., students) are asked to react to a problem or situation in the way that they think appropriate for their assigned role. For example, members of a social studies class might role-play the reactions of various members of a community to some important issue.

Several factors will contribute to a successful experience with role-playing. First, it must be clear to the role-players not only what role they are taking, but the behaviors appropriate for that role. For example, if a history teacher wants his students to role-play a discussion of democracy among Jefferson, Paine, George III, and Rousseau, then these persons' ideas obviously must be understood. Secondly, students will often require considerable support in playing their roles enthusiastically and convincingly—particularly before the climate for this type of activity has been established. Thirdly, students should be assigned to roles which suit the learning objectives of the lesson. For example, if a teacher wants students to play roles which are counter to their true beliefs, he will have to determine what those beliefs are, as well as the students' abilities to play their roles.

6. Small groups

The potential for involving students in learning through the use of small groups is indeed great. You can think of small groups as two students or more. The small group offers an increased chance for participation for each member of the group compared to the regular classroom group. Two important behaviors are required of a teacher if groups are to provide suitable conditions for motivation and learning. First, the members of the group need to be clear as to their purpose for being (i.e., the objectives should be clarified); second, the group should have a clear idea about how to proceed toward its objectives.

7. Activity

The final strategy simply emphasizes the nature of participation. Any activity—manipulating pulleys instead of observing the teacher or only reading about them; constructing and/or experimenting with a wind tunnel; going outside the school for participation in some social or political experience—which is appropriate to your learning objectives will generally enhance motivation. While it is possible for activities to interfere with efficient learning procedures and for teaching to become so activity centered that important principles and concepts are not taught, such cases are, in the authors' estimation, quite rare. It is, of course, important that students be aware of the objectives of participation in the activity and generally that they have the opportunity to discuss their observations and what was learned.

OBSERVATION FORM[1]

The observation form for motivation focuses on students. With the information provided by the use of this observation procedure, you can determine the effect of your motivation strategy on the students you teach. There are four broad categories of behavior defined below.

Category	Description
Participation	Student volunteers information. Responds enthusiastically. Takes part in activity with obvious interest or enjoyment.
Attention	Student does assigned work. Responds when called on. Pays attention to teacher and class.
Inattention	Does not pay attention. Daydreams. Looks around room, Fidgets in seat. Does not respond when called on. Engages in inappropriate but not obstructive activity.
Obstruction	Makes inappropriate noise or disrupts class. Interferes with other students' work. Refuses to do assignment. Attempts to get teacher or class off topic.

Observation Procedure

With these categories, you may observe the attentive/inattentive behaviors of individual students during a lesson. Using a stop watch or a watch with a sweep hand, code behavior at fifteen-second intervals. On the observation sheet, make a check mark next to the appropriate category. If more than one type of behavior occurs during the fifteen-second interval, estimate which category occupied the greatest part of the interval and check it. After you have coded an individual student's behavior for one minute, begin observing another student. Continuing this procedure for the duration of the lesson will provide a sample of the attentive/inattentive behaviors of students. (Note to teacher: You may find it instructive to estimate the amounts of the different behaviors in your lesson before checking with the observer. The degree of correspondence between your own estimate and the observed estimate will give you an indication of how accurately you are perceiving.)

[1] You may wish to refer back to the observation form in chapter 2, on page 22, for use in this lesson.

Observation Form for Motivation

Check the appropriate category every fifteen seconds. Rotate to a different student after each minute.

	1	2	3	4	1	2	3	4	1	2	3	4	1	2	3	4	1	2	3	4
Participation																				
Attention																				
Inattention																				
Obstruction																				

	1	2	3	4	1	2	3	4	1	2	3	4	1	2	3	4	1	2	3	4
Participation																				
Attention																				
Inattention																				
Obstruction																				

	1	2	3	4	1	2	3	4	1	2	3	4	1	2	3	4	1	2	3	4
Participation																				
Attention																				
Inattention																				
Obstruction																				

	1	2	3	4	1	2	3	4	1	2	3	4	1	2	3	4	1	2	3	4
Participation																				
Attention																				
Inattention																				
Obstruction																				

MOTIVATING: LESSON FOR ANALYSIS AND EVALUATION

First Lesson (beginning)

LESSON	ANALYSIS
T: We all know there are seven continents on the globe. What would you think if I told you there was an eighth? Let's just imagine for a little while that there are eight continents, and the eighth one you get to make up—you get to create. If you want to have one that has forests or mountains or beaches, you are going to put it in there; you are going to construct a continent. Here I have paper and pencils. Do you all want to try a continent? You'd better take three pieces of paper. (All students take paper and pencil.) Okay, first of all, think about what you want on your continent. What's the first thing? S: Beaches. T: Okay, beaches. What do you want? S2: Fresh water. T: Okay, and you? S3: Beaches, forests, and mountains. T: Okay. Now, how are we going to put these on the map? Let's all just start drawing our maps and see how we do.	Divergent problem presented—may arouse curiosity. Initial statement of objective. Activity planned to involve every student. Teacher uses divergent question to stimulate participation. Student responses are encouraged by being accepted. Students are involved individually in the activity. Expression of different student ideas is provided for. Objective will probably need further clarification.

Second Lesson (beginning)

T: Today you were supposed to read the chapter on totalitarian governments. Have you all read it? Linda, can you tell me the six methods of coercion that most totalitarian governments use? Well, haven't you read the chapter? L (Linda): No. T: (yelling) Well, what were you doing? Why haven't you read it? I assigned it—what's wrong? L: I don't know. I just didn't have time.	Recall expected of student. Teacher seems to be threatening students. Student may not have read chapter, or she may be resisting teacher's authority. Negative reinforcement.

LESSON	ANALYSIS
T: Well, I want you to come in after school today, and I want you to write an essay on each one of these reasons—the methods of coercion. And I don't want this to happen again, because if it does, I'm going to call your parents and I'm going to see that you do this. I assigned that chapter and I want all of you to read it.	Teacher coerces student.
I'm sure a lot of other people in here haven't read that. Now I know Gretchen and Mac—they're good students—they probably have read it.	Unjustified praise. May be negatively reinforcing.
(At this point the teacher hesitates, composes himself and asks, "What have I been doing? How would you describe how I have been acting?" A discussion of authoritarian behavior and totalitarian governments follows.)	Use of a shock strategy revealed. This appears to be an extremely creative and effective introduction to the topic of the characteristics of totalitarianism.

Third Lesson (selected parts)

LESSON	ANALYSIS
T: Today we'll just answer a few questions and maybe you can pick up something as we go along. Who would like to volunteer an answer for Adolf Hitler—I mean give some identification of him—who he was, a little bit of his background and where he sits in history? Would anyone like to do this?	Condescending attitude toward students. No clear objective.
S: He was the leader of Germany right before and during World War II. He thought the German race was superior to all others.	
T: Would anyone like to add to this, especially the point of the German people being superior? What went along with this? Would anyone like to add to this content?	Divergent question. However, teacher seems to be trying to get at a specific point, but students are unclear about it. An inappropriate use of divergent questions. Students are not being reinforced for attempting to participate.
S: Well, he tried to purify it.	
T: Yes, and what actions were taken to do this? How many were eliminated during his reign? Anyone care to guess?	
S: A million.	
T: No.	
S: Two million?	

LESSON	ANALYSIS
T: No about six million. About six million Jews. This was one of his primary ways to purify the German race. Does anyone else wish to add more about Adolf Hitler? (Silence)	Extending questions and problem structuring would be better strategies.
Well, you can get the rest out of your text. Does anyone care to say anything about the Weimer Republic? No one knows? (Short lecture on Weimar Republic follows)	Little interest shown by teacher for the content.
Now, does anyone know anything about Bismarck? Well . . . (Short lecture on Bismarck follows)	
Now, the next time we meet, we'll go on discussing those other items, and I suggest you read the text before the next period. I may give a pop test next time.	No objective. Inappropriate use of the word "discussing." Vague assignment and implied threat.

Fourth Lesson

T: Class, you remember yesterday when we discussed what it meant to be scientific, that one very important thing was to be careful observers. Can anyone tell why that's important—to observe carefully?	Question used to evaluate previous learning and to determine readiness for new learning.
S: Well, if you don't, you might miss something.	
T: Right. Why do you think it is important not to miss anything? Joe?	Question for justification used to extend response.
S: Because science tries to find out what causes things to happen and if you don't see something and that was the cause then you wouldn't know it.	
T: That's a very good reason for observing carefully. You want to make sure you don't overlook the real cause why something actually occurred. Can you think of any other reasons for careful observation? (silence)	Postive reinforcement of student's response. Further reinforced by having teacher build on student's idea.
Well, let me give you an example. Suppose you had a room in your house that didn't have any doors or windows, and you knew something was inside but you didn't know what was in the room.	Problem presented to focus attention and arouse curiosity.
S: You have to listen so that you can find out what was in there.	
T: But suppose you told me what you thought was in there, and I didn't believe you. Then what would you do? Anybody?	Teacher challenges students for better response —automatic positive reinforcement is not given.

LESSON	ANALYSIS
S: Well, he could show you how he made his observations and then you could make them too and find out if he was right.	
T: That's exactly it! And that's another reason for careful observation: so that someone else can use the same procedure and get the same results as you.	Good positive reinforcement.
T: Okay, today we are going to observe carefully (picks up shoe box from desk). What do you suppose is in this box?	Past and present learning experiences are related. Beginning of an objective, but will need further clarification. Surprising question—curiosity aroused.
S: Shoes. (laughter)	
T: Well, could be. You observed the label on the box and made a reasonable hypothesis about the contents. How could you tell for sure?	Student's response accepted and probed for extension.
S: Open it up.	
T: Okay. Right. But notice that the lid is taped onto the box so you can't open it and look. Is there any other way to observe the contents without looking inside?	
S: Shake it.	
T: (Shakes box.)	
S: It's not shoes.	
T: Doesn't sound like shoes, does it? Okay, now I've got seven boxes here and each one is sealed so you can't look inside it. You'll have to observe the contents of the box some other way besides opening it up. Okay, you will need to determine what is in the box by observing carefully, and keep a record of your observations so that once you decide what is inside, you can prove it to someone else. Since there are seven boxes, four of you can work together on each box to try to figure out what is inside. Get into your groups now and I'll distribute a box to each group.	Objective clarified. Sufficient material and grouping used to involve most students in the activity. Use of group work apparently common—which helps minimize the distraction of forming into groups.
(Students form groups of four.)	
S: Does each box have the same thing in it?	
T: You'll have to figure that out yourself.	
S: When will we find out?	
T: That depends. When you are sure that you know what is in there, and can show the class why you are sure, and they can say that your observations are complete enough.	Criteria of acceptable group performance are clarified. This seems exciting—some competition involved.

LESSON	ANALYSIS
(Students are in groups.) T: Okay. Before I pass out the boxes, let's make sure things are straight. You need to observe what is in the box. And you must keep a record of what observations you make and why you made them. You should write it down. Then when you think you know what is in the box, your group can report it to the class. If the class agrees that your observations and procedures were okay, then you can open it and verify your hypotheses. But if we don't think the observations were enough, that you overlooked something, then you will have to keep at it. (Teacher summarizes procedure on board.) Fair enough? S: Will we find out today what's inside? T: Maybe, maybe not. If you don't today, then there will be more time later. S: Can we do anything we want? T: Except open the box. I'll come around to your groups and ask you questions and you can ask me questions about what you are doing. Remember, keep a record of what you do. Okay. (Students start working.)	Activity and objective further clarified. Important that groups are clear about their task. Opportunity for teacher to individualize instruction.

MOTIVATING: SUGGESTED ACTIVITIES

1. Discipline simulation. During your lab lesson on motivating, or as a supplementary lesson, students can simulate different types of inappropriate classroom behavior. These inappropriate behaviors might include: aggressive behavior toward the teacher and/or students; resistance or delaying; noise-making or other inappropriate attention-seeking behavior; withdrawal, etc.

Some strategies you may wish to use in attempting to deal effectively with such behavior include: removal and isolation of an aggressive student, punishment, nonreinforcement (ignoring), providing a wider range of learning activities, establishing clearly defined objectives for students, defining the limits of appropriate behavior, reinforcing appropriate behavior, discussing with students the reasons for their behaviors, etc.

When discipline problems are being simulated in the laboratory, most students (including colleagues who are pupils) are not content with one or two instances of inappropriate behavior. When misbehavior is sanctioned, there is a strong tendency for it to persist. Therefore, it may be necessary for the lab instructor to place limits on the number and kinds of incidents which are simulated during any one lesson.

An important part of this laboratory lesson is subsequent discussion of your own reactions toward different types of student behavior, and how you felt about your own behavior and that of your students. A video or audio tape recording of the lesson will facilitate self-appraisal, as will feedback from your instructor and colleagues.

2. The films, "Walls," "Less Far Than The Arrow," and "I Walk Away in the Rain," from the Critical Moments in Teaching film series (Holt, Rinehart, and Winston, Inc., 1968) present three different aspects of the problem of motivation. If you view one or more of these, consider what motivating strategies *you* might try if faced with the same problems as those presented in the films.

3. In conjunction with the task of motivating, it would be appropriate to devote time to the variety of ways that audio-visual resources can be used in the classroom (and laboratory). Commonly used resources include overhead and opaque projectors, transparencies, films and slides, tape recorders, dry-mounted and laminated visual materials, and record players.

Learning appropriate use of audio-visual resources might be arranged during a special audio-visual laboratory. This lab can be designed to give you experience in preparing materials and operating audio-visual equipment.

4. Along with a consideration of what you can do as a teacher to stimulate student interest and participation, you might also consider what interests you about teaching. Following are two exercises which may help you explore this area of your own motivation. You may wish to compare your reactions with those of your colleagues and discuss the factors that underlie your reactions.

a. Rate each of the items below according to your perception of its importance as a factor in motivating you to want to teach. Rate 1 ("very important") to 7 ("of no importance") or rank the items from most to the least important.

1. I find studying my subject area satisfying.
2. I find (or expect to find) working with children or adolescents satisfying.
3. Teachers I have admired have been influential in my decision to become a teacher.
4. I believe I influence (or will be able to influence) students to become better persons.
5. Teaching offers security and assurance of a job.
6. Teaching offers a career in which I feel I can succeed.
7. Teaching is about the only occupation I have ever seriously considered.
8. (Other reasons)

b. The check list below describes possible motivating characteristics of your teaching. Based on your previous lessons in the lab, determine the five which you feel are most descriptive of your teaching, and those which you feel are least descriptive. Then give the original list to several persons who have participated in or observed your lessons, and ask them to check their perceptions of the five most and five least descriptive terms for your teaching.

____ enthusiastic

____ warm, friendly

____ interesting lessons

____ encouraged participation

____ clear objectives, expectations

____ students actually learned something

____ praised and reinforced

____ variety of procedures used

____ used A-V aids

____ aroused curiosity

____ made purpose of lesson clear

____ involved students

____ gave feedback

5. References:

The following chapter offers specific suggestions which may help you deal effectively with "discipline problems:" "Discipline in Classroom Practice" by Fritz Redl in *When We Deal With Children,* New York: The Free Press, 1966, pp. 254-300.

For a highly readable analysis of the use of reinforcement in the classroom read, "Why Teachers Fail" by B. F. Skinner, *Saturday Review,* October 16, 1965, pp. 98ff. Also reprinted in *Readings in Educational Psychology,* edited by

H.W. Bernard and W.C. Huckins, Scranton, Penn: International Textbook Co. 1967, pp. 432-44.

For an account of how a teacher effectively built on the life experiences of her pupils, read *Teacher* by Sylvia Aston-Warner, New York: Simon and Schuster, 1963.

An interesting observation procedure—"shadow study" (observing a pupil throughout the school day)—and discomforting data on what the average school day is like for many high school pupils are included in *The High School We Saw: One Day in the Eighth Grade,* by John H. Lounsbury and Jean V. Marani, Washington: Association for Supervision and Curriculum Development, 1964.

Several ideas for individualizing instruction within the classroom and in the overall school curriculum are included in *Individualizing Learning Through Modular-Flexible Programming,* ed. Baynor Petrequin, New York: McGraw-Hill Book Co., 1968.

chapter 6

Evaluating

Evaluating consists of determining what students have learned as a result of your teaching. When you complete this task, you will have completed the last basic teaching task. From now on all of your lessons in the teaching laboratory will involve aspects of the four basic teaching tasks. However, they will not unfold neatly in a one-to-four sequence; rather they will be interrelated in complex ways not always distinguishable from one another.

Although evaluating is often viewed as one of the more unpleasant tasks of teaching (often associated only with the difficult job of assigning grades to students), this need not be the case. Evaluation can and should be intimately related to all aspects of teaching; it should not be treated as a formal, separate activity. For example, evaluating is closely related to determining readiness. The information gained minute by minute on how well pupils are doing may tell you both what they have learned and how ready they are for the next stage of instruction. Also, determining readiness before instruction has begun can represent evaluating if you are looking back at the results of previous instruction. Likewise, evaluation can be viewed as part of determining readiness if you are looking forward to the next sequence of instruction.

Evaluating is also closely related to clarifying objectives. If you evaluate appropriately, you evaluate in terms of the objectives of your teaching. In addition, the evidence on how well your objectives are being achieved is also evidence to use for setting new objectives. Evaluation should help clarify your objectives by being consistent with them. Unfortunately, this is not always the case. Take, for example, the student who ignores what the teacher is saying (possibly about the objectives of the lesson) in order to study the questions at the end of the chapter. Why? Because that's where the test questions always come from!

Motivation and evaluation affect one another. Motivation can be increased or decreased by evaluation. If evaluating is used only to grade students and not to help them improve their understanding, then it may decrease motivation for those pupils who receive the lower grades. The appropriateness of the motivation provided for students with the higher grades can be questioned if it is the only source of motivation. On the other hand, when the information gained through evaluation is used to set appropriate objectives for pupils, and the path to satisfactory performance is made clear, this should not hinder motivation. Viewing this relationship the other way around, evaluation is affected by motivation. If motivation is high, the learning associated with evaluation activities and the information gained from them should be enhanced.

From these comments on the interrelationships between evaluation and the other basic teaching tasks, it should be clear that the task of evaluating is closely bound up in determining readiness, clarifying objectives, and motivating. In addition to providing you and your students with feedback about their performance, evaluating also gives you evidence for judging your own performance, that is, the effectiveness of your teaching strategies. For example, whenever you find you must give a student an "F" or an "A" it may well be that you can give yourself the grade along with the student!

Evaluating in the teaching laboratory consists of evaluating while you are teaching, that is, gaining information about the progress of your pupils during your lesson. To do this you must provide some means during the lessons for students to demonstrate their progress toward your objectives. For instance, if you are teaching a lesson on weights and measures, you must ask some questions during the lesson or provide time for demonstrating comprehension to see how well the learning objectives regarding weights and measures are being achieved. If you are teaching students an interpretation of a poem, the jump shot in basketball, experimental procedures in chemistry, or the computation of the area of a rectangle, you must in each case allow students to actually attempt the task as you teach the lesson. By the time you end your lesson, you should have a good idea as to the effects of your teaching.

A second aspect of evaluating may be developed in relation to the teaching laboratory, that is to use the lab as a place to try out formal, post-instructional measures of achievement—for example, written tests and assignments. To do this you will have your lab students actually take your test or complete your assignment after you have finished your lab lesson. Of course time will have to be provided for this, and probably no more than about ten minutes should be required to complete any one test or assignment. When you receive the results of your evaluation, you may "correct" them and even assign grades to your lab students.

The levels of performance for evaluating are presented in the evaluation and feedback guide. If this task is treated as two parts—evaluating during the lesson and evaluating after the lesson has been completed—then these criteria should be applied separately to each part.

EVALUATING: EVALUATION AND FEEDBACK GUIDE

TEACHER'S NAME _____ RATER'S NAME _____ DATE _____

CRITERIA	COMMENTS
IV. Evaluating	

1. Excellent. No real weaknesses. Relevant information was gained from all pupils. The teacher either gained information or, through an assignment or prepared test, provided the basis for gaining information about the extent to which pupils had achieved the objectives of the lesson.

2. Good. At least one identifiable weakness. Much relevant information was gained.

3. Acceptable. Some important information was not gained, but in general the teacher has enough information to judge whether he can go on to other objectives.

4. Serious weakness. The teacher failed to determine what was learned and/or what serious learning problems existed which would hinder further instruction.

5. Vague attention to task. Many weaknesses. Little relevant information was gained.

6. No attention to task. No relevant information was gained.

BASIC TEACHING TASKS

I.	Determining Readiness	1 2 3 4 5 6
II.	Clarifying Objectives	1 2 3 4 5 6
III.	Motivating	1 2 3 4 5 6
IV.	Evaluating	1 2 3 4 5 6

STRATEGIES FOR EVALUATING

Strategies for evaluating will be classified in two ways: those dealing with evaluating during a lab lesson (concurrent with teaching) and those which are appropriate to use after your lesson has been completed.

Strategies for Evaluating During Instruction[1]

Questioning

Again we mention what is possibly the teacher's most versatile tool—the question. Questions are used in evaluating to determine the extent to which pupils have achieved an objective. It is important to remember that one student's ability to answer a question correctly does not necessarily indicate that all or even most of your class can do likewise. In using questions to evaluate, it is important to call on many pupils, including those who may not know the answer.

Another important point is that your questions should reflect your objectives. If your objectives are to have students interpret a document and apply it to a current situation, don't ask students to recall what was contained in the document (they should have the document in their hands). Likewise, answers to the question, "In your own words, tell what an equation is," could be used to assess whether students understood the concept "equation," but not to determine whether students could use an equation to solve a problem. For a more detailed description of questioning strategies, it should be useful to review the discussion of questioning in chapter 3.

Observing Student Performance

Many kinds of objectives require other than verbal types of performance to evaluate their attainment. For example, if you want to see how well someone can drive a car, you don't usually ask them to tell you about driving—you observe them actually driving (although you may want a certain amount of verbalization before you accompany them on the highway!). Likewise, if students are to solve an equation, compute a percentage, hem a dress, perform the backstroke, sketch a profile, or dissect a frog, you will probably evaluate these objectives by observing students performing these activities. Thus, to evaluate student attainment of nonverbal behaviors, you need to provide a situation in which students can demonstrate the appropriate behaviors.

As was the case with the use of questioning, observing student performance should include as many students in the class as possible. The performance that is used for evaluation should, of course, reflect the objectives of the lesson.

Many objectives include both verbal and nonverbal components. For these objectives, evaluating during instruction should include both aspects. Thus, the

[1]You should review the strategies for determining readiness (chapter 3).

objective for solving some type of equation may include specifying reasons for each step of the process. Appropriate evaluation would include observing pupil performance (i.e., solving equations) and questioning to find out if students understood what they were doing.

Student Evaluation

Another type of evaluation that may be used concurrently with instruction is self-assessment. This means that the pupils themselves develop questions or procedures to determine what they have learned. For instance, you might ask students to write two questions which deal with the most important functions of the three branches of the federal government. Individual students or groups of students could write these questions. Students could answer their own questions, or exchange questions to be answered by others, or justify their questions importance. Pupils could also develop criteria for judging the adequacy of their questions or answers, write questions which would indicate what should have been learned during a lesson or unit, or questions reflecting what was important to them. Use of this strategy will also enable the students to learn from each other and to obtain feedback and reinforcement for their own questioning behavior from both the teacher and other students.

As you can see, evaluating strategies are bound up with instruction. These strategies can be as exciting and effective as your instructional strategies. For example, evaluating strategies can even involve aspects of discovery exercises, role-playing, debate, dramatic performance, and experimentation.

Strategies for Evaluating After Instruction

These strategies will be reviewed briefly. For more information on the specifics of test construction and evaluation, you should refer to the activities listed at the end of this chapter.

Completion tests

These tests are usually limited in their use to the assessment of recall. They include tests which ask for short answers to questions; the listing of information, e.g., three parts of a flower; the completion of sentences; and the identification or definition of given phenomena.

True-false tests

The true-false test is often used to assess recall, although it can be constructed to evaluate several types of objectives. The more complex the true-false statement becomes, the greater the likelihood of ambiguity, that is, students will attend to the unimportant part of the statement. Allowing the student to give a reason for his choice will provide additional information for these and other forced-choice tests.

Matching and Arrangement tests

These tests require that phenomena be associated with one another or arranged in some particular order (e.g., chronological or logical). If well constructed, they can be used to evaluate several types of objectives (recall, comprehension, interpretation, application, etc.). For example, students could be asked to match twenty descriptions and application statements with five general concepts.

Multiple-choice tests

These tests require that one of several responses to a question be selected as correct, or that the "best" or "worst" response be selected. The questions can also be preceded by information (graphs, stories, data, etc.) to which responses are related. If carefully constructed, this type of test can be used to evaluate with maximum objectivity most educational objectives that do not require written or other performance measures.

Essay tests

These tests take less time to construct but more time to evaluate than multiple-choice tests. They are appropriate for evaluating educational objectives in which written expression is important. They are also important whenever a personalized response is desired, e.g., an interpretation or an opinion. One difficulty with the use of essay tests is establishing suitable performance criteria. To grade an essay test you should be as explicit as possible regarding the criteria and levels of performance which you consider important. Of course these should be communicated to the students before they take the tests so they know what is expected of them.

Student-made tests

This strategy is particularly appropriate for unit or chapter tests. It provides a useful review for students who, individually or in groups, can be asked to construct questions for the test. Because students, in attempting to make difficult questions, diverge widely from your instructional objectives, you should give them some idea as to what you consider important before they construct their questions. It is also important to give them feedback on the kinds of questions you eventually select.

Oral tests

All of the tests described thus far can be constructed as oral tests. Oral tests take considerable time, yet they provide a degree of personalization which is not possible in a written test. An oral test will give you more appropriate feedback from students who cannot read and/or write well—unless, of course, you are assessing reading and writing. In addition, oral tests will be particularly appropriate when oral skills are being assessed, e.g., giving a speech or conversing in a foreign language.

Assignments

Instead of giving a test immediately after your lab lesson, you may choose to give an assignment. The assignment may involve a written task (an essay) or a performance task (solving problems or practicing a song). The assignment should clearly reflect the objectives of your lesson, and the students should understand its purpose. Since students will not do the assignment in the laboratory, you should determine whether they feel that they have had sufficient instruction to complete the assignment on their own.

In determining which strategies to choose for evaluation, you should consider which one most appropriately evaluates the objectives you are attempting to accomplish. Since a "test" is itself a learning experience, it should be consistent with your objectives and should contribute to their attainment.

As a final thought, you might benefit by considering once again the two-sided nature of evaluation. All of the evaluating strategies described give you not only information relative to your pupils' achievement, but evidence on which to evaluate the effectiveness of your teaching.

OBSERVATION FORM: EVALUATING

The purpose of this observation instrument is to code the frequency of two types of student behavior during a lesson: verbal behavior (VB) and nonverbal behavior (NVB). The behavior of each pupil is coded on a series of divided rectangles such as the following:

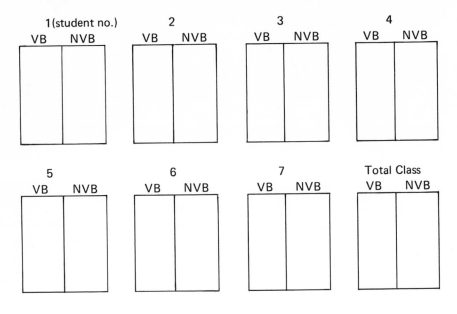

Each rectangle represents a student in the class, and it may facilitate coding to arrange the rectangles on a separate sheet according to the classroom seating arrangement. A check mark should be placed in a student's column under verbal behavior whenever the student answers a question, asks a question, or initiates a statement based on the content of lesson. Whenever a student exhibits a nonverbal behavior—writes on the board, operates a typewriter, manipulates an experimental apparatus, or any other nonverbal behavior which is relevant to achieving the lesson objective—then that behavior is coded by a check mark in the column for nonverbal behavior. If most or all students respond verbally or perform at the same time, then a check is made in the column labeled "total class."

Coding during a lesson should begin only when actual instruction toward some objective has begun. If the objective is not specifically stated, or if you cannot tell whether a behavior can be useful for evaluation, then you should use the following decision rule: begin coding when student statements, questions, or responses depend on some idea, problem, or content which has been *introduced* in the lesson by the teacher.

You may use information from this form to determine the extent to which each student participated during a lesson (and therefore provided some information important to evaluation). This is important because instruction that proceeds after evaluating the learning of only one or a few students (often the most knowledgeable) will bypass most of the class.

You may also use the instrument as a check against the ratings you receive on the criteria of evaluation. Low ratings may indicate that you are not obtaining enough information about student performance to determine if learning occurred, and the frequency and distribution of tallies on the coding sheet may confirm this.

EVALUATING: LESSONS FOR ANALYSIS AND EVALUATION

(The following lesson segment occurred after a presentation and discussion of characterization in which one objective was that students should be able to state or show how different characters in plays and stories feel.)

LESSON	ANALYSIS
T: Soon we will be reading *The Glass Menagerie* by Tennessee Williams. This play is about the deep emotions of several of the very different characters in the play. I want you to try to empathize with the characters in the play—to feel like you think they really feel. Now we are going to try an experiment on how well each of us can empathize. (Holds up small sack.)	Statement of objective.
In this bag are objects—a lot of different things—and I want you to take one of them. These are things we use a lot and we don't usually think of them as having feelings, but I want you to pretend that they do, and I want you to try to act like you think this object feels.	Unusual strategy; arouses and involves students in lesson.
Now don't be afraid—nobody is going to judge you. It's going to be your own interpretation of how your object feels. Do you understand the importance of doing this? If you can feel for a tube of toothpaste, then you can certainly feel for the characters in *The Glass Menagerie.* Do you agree with that?	Reason for activity is clarified—question used for evaluation, results in response asking for clarification.
S: Can we talk while we're doing it?	Student apparently feels apprehension about the task.
T: Oh yes, you may talk and act—anything to express the feeling you think the object might have. (Noise and laughter from the class.) You may do whatever you feel like.	
All right, let me give you an example. But don't pattern yourself after me if you don't want to. Feel free to do it anyway you want. I'll just give an example of how I would interpret . . . okay, I'll reach into the bag and . . . here's a tube of glue. You never thought of glue as having feelings. Now I'll show you what I think it must feel like to be glue—not the tube but glue. (Teacher clasps her arms around her waist and with accompanying facial contortions starts to pull and stretch with her arms.)	Teacher attempts to clarify further to reduce apprehension. Good use of example—teacher is willing to do what is expected of students.
T: Does that make sense to you? (Laughter) Okay, who wants to be second?	

LESSON	ANALYSIS
(Girl volunteers to try a comb. She moves her hand over hair as though she is combing it.)	Performance assessed by observation.
T: You're combing your hair, right? But show us how you think the comb might feel. When you comb your hair, how does the comb feel?	Student's first example used to clarify the task.
S: Oh. I see what you mean now. (Student walks jerkily across room, breathing heavily.)	Student performance here cannot be used to evaluate directly whether students can empathize with "human" characters; teacher must assume that ability to displace their own feelings to inanimate objects is related to empathy.
T: Can anyone tell us what that comb feels? What is she showing us?	
S: The hair is tangled and it's tough to get through. She has to work hard to do it.	
T: How does she feel about it?	
S: Tired.	Student probably feels much more successful in her second portrayal. These student performances provide the evidence for judging the ability of the students to engage in this activity.
T: Okay, Jan, is that what you were trying to show?	
S: Yes.	
(Various students proceed to portray a letter opener, toothpaste, lipstick, sponge, and a flower.)	
T: Okay, let's go back to the initial idea behind this experiment—to feel for the characters in the play we are about to read. Remember how important empathy is—some of these characters may be as different from you as the tube of lipstick was for Mike. As you read the play tonight I want you to think about this, and be ready tomorrow to tell, or maybe portray, what the different characters are like.	Original objective is re-emphasized. (Involvement in the activity could lead students to forget the objective.) Assignment used to extend the learning. Results—"telling or portraying"—will provide evidence on the success of the portrayal activity and the assignment.

(The following lesson segment occurred during a unit on communication. An objective of the unit is the development of listening skills, aspects of which include restating and summarizing what others have said and differentiating between statements which express feeling and those which mainly express ideas, and are neutral in feeling.)

LESSON	ANALYSIS
T: We've been working at listening to what others say. Bob, would you review for us what we can listen for when someone tries to communicate?	Question used to evaluate previous learning.
S: Well, what he says. What idea he is trying to get across.	Prior learning reinforced.
T: Yes. That's very important. Anything else we should listen for?	Interaction used to evaluate, reinforce, and review prior learning necessary for continuation of instruction.
S: Well, lots of times when people speak they communicate more than just an idea. I mean they have some feelings or emotion in what they say.	
T: Right. Can anyone give an example of this?	
(Discussion continues for several minutes.)	
T: Okay. Let's find out now how well you do listen. I'll play this song—it's a folk song—and you can see how many questions you can answer about it. Just listen and I'll have some questions after it's over.	No evidence that this folk song is of particular interest to students—may be an engaging activity.
(Teacher plays the song on a tape recorder)	
Okay, here are the questions. See if you can answer these. (Questions are distributed to each student.)	

1.   The song as a whole is about:
    a. a prisoner and his plans for escape
    b. a singer telling of his accomplishments
    c. an unhappy man and his problem with his girl friend
2.   The feeling in the song can best be described as:
    a. optimistic
    b. neutral
    c. pessimistic
3.   The main character in the folk song is thinking of leaving for:
    a. Alabama
    b. Alberta
    c. Alaska
4.   In his new location he plans to:
    a. seek new evidence and help for his case
    b. sing with a traveling group
    c. work for friends
5.   In the end, the man states that he:
    a. will never return to this place again

Multiple-choice test used during lesson to assess listening objectives. Are the feelings and ideas components equally represented?

LESSON	ANALYSIS
b. will return after he has secured legal help	
c. will look for his friend if he ever comes back	
(The correct answers to the questions are presented and briefly discussed.)	Some feedback provided.
T: Now, keep the song and the correct answers in mind while I present to you some ideas about different things to listen to. These ideas will help you analyze a point of view or argument. When I finish with this explanation, I'm going to ask you to take a short quiz which will cover the points I'm going to make. All of the questions will also involve the folk song we just heard.	Additional instruction given to extend listening skills.
S: Do we get to hear the record again?	
T: All right, I'll play it again in a minute if you still feel you need to hear it. If you listen carefully to what I'm going to say, I think you'll remember enough of the song to be able to answer the questions. (A presentation is given which draws a distinction between listening for *ideas* and listening for *feelings*. Attention is also drawn to the difference between "clarifying" and "supporting" an idea. Some interaction is involved in which examples are drawn from the folk song. The song is played again.)	New listening objectives are introduced.
T: All right. Now I'd like you to complete this short quiz to see how well you listened and can apply the information I've just presented. (The following quiz is distributed to students.)	
1. Give a one sentence definition of "an idea" and a one sentence definition of "a feeling."	Quiz including several types of questions is used to evaluate learning, after the lesson is completed.
2. Mark (I) for each of the following sentences which are mainly expressions of ideas and (F) for those which are mainly expressions of feelings.	
He is going to Alberta.	
He is depressed over a broken relationship.	
He will work for friends.	
He is unhappy about leaving.	
3. "He is going to Alberta as soon as possible to escape the situation he is in." This sentence represents (check one):	
a. clarification of an idea.	
b. support of an idea.	
c. both (a) and (b).	
4. Short answer (two short paragraphs). Describe the main "idea" and the "feeling tone" of the folk song played in class.	

EVALUATING: SUGGESTED ACTIVITIES

1. One objection to the use of essay tests is the difficulty in obtaining reliable evaluation. Along with your colleagues, grade an essay and write comments about it. Then compare and discuss the assigned grades and comments.

2. Score, return, and discuss with the lab students the test you gave them. Determine whether they thought it reflected your objectives and whether your expectations of how students would perform matched reality.

3. For useful information on constructing and evaluating classroom tests, examine the materials available from Educational Testing Service (Princeton, N.J.): "Making the Classroom Test: A Guide for Teachers," "Multiple-Choice Questions: A Close Look," and "Short-Cut Statistics for Teacher-Made Tests." See also educational psychology texts, which generally contain a chapter or two on test construction and interpretation.

4. Questioning is an important strategy for evaluation during instruction, and you need to develop proficiency in asking questions. Working with a colleague, state several important objectives that you might teach toward, and then ask questions which would evaluate attainment of these objectives.

5. Based on your assessment of student performance in this lesson, plan another laboratory lesson in which you provide feedback to students about their performance. Also plan any additional instruction needed to improve student attainment of objectives.

6. For an exercise which emphasizes an often-ignored source of information, you may wish to participate in a nonverbal communication experience. For example, you may spend a few minutes in pairs observing one another's facial expressions and gestures, attempting to assess the feelings of the other person. Or you might attempt to carry on a "conversation" using only gestures. Also, "periods of observation" can be used in the lab. These would require that you stop your lesson, take a few seconds to observe your students, and attempt to express their reactions.

part 3

LEARNING TASKS

Thus far we have emphasized teaching tasks which are independent of particular kinds of learning objectives or subject fields. For example, you have been asked to clarify objectives regardless of whether your lesson was to deal with the structure of language, a scientific principle, or the exploration of a problem. The same principle has held for determining readiness, for motivating, and for evaluating.

The tasks in this section have a different focus. These tasks are concerned with particular kinds of learning objectives, comprising four categories: (1) concepts and principles, (2) problem-solving, (3) attitudes, and (4) skills.

In each of the next four chapters these learning objectives and related strategies are described. Your task is to select from among the strategies and use them to accomplish the particular type of learning objective in your lesson.

There is an alternative to these four learning tasks (or a supplement if you have sufficient time). The alternative is presented in chapter 11, "Learning Objectives." This chapter is a guide to a self-directed, independent approach to the problem of categorizing learning objectives and generating appropriate teaching strategies. This self-directed task may be viewed as a summary experience in the teaching laboratory after the learning tasks have been completed, or it may serve as a point of immediate departure toward a series of lessons, comprising unique objectives and strategies.

Before proceeding to the learning tasks, we feel it important to discuss a problem which often arises at this point in the teaching laboratory. Just as the "motivating" task has been observed to be a common point for intense interest and learning on the part of lab teachers, this point in the lab has been observed as a common point for many where interest and learning wane. Some teachers have learned to "survive" in the lab and are satisfied with maintaining a minimal level of performance. Others have reported that, although they still want to improve their teaching ability, they don't feel the lab experience is any longer contributing to their improvement.

We don't intend to imply that the above descriptions fit all lab teachers. Many feel they are still continuing to make steady improvement in the lab, and others are just beginning to make their own "break throughs."

We believe the key factor in making the laboratory a positive learning experience, as well as in maintaining its value, involves individualized, constructive feedback. If teachers are getting feedback from their colleagues, pupils, and instructor which relates directly to their identification of teaching strengths and weaknesses and suggestions for improvement, then we believe that this will go far in maintaining the lab as a positive learning environment.

In addition to individualized, constructive feedback, the introduction of new experiences contributes to the continuing effectiveness of the lab. For example, at this point lab teachers may begin to plan and teach in teams of two or more, new lab groups may be formed, and new kinds of feedback, such as video equipment, may be introduced.

Whatever your next step in the teaching lab (team-teaching, learning concepts and principles, a unique task), you will be building on your previous learning. The basic teaching tasks will continue to be relevant dimensions in your subsequent lessons.

chapter 7

Concepts and Principles

Your objective in this lesson is to teach a concept or principle, using either a "discovery" or an "expository" strategy. Regardless of the strategy used, you should aim for student understanding, as evidenced by the students' ability to state in their own words the appropriate principle or concept and/or to apply this learning to a new problem.

A *concept* may be defined as the label associated with a class of objects, where "objects" refers to any group of things having a common characteristic. If a student has learned a concept, then he is able to identify things which are, and which are not, examples of the concept. He should also be able to state the common characteristic(s) or attribute(s) of the class of objects which identify the concept. For example, understanding of the concept "prime number" would be indicated if a student could identify prime and nonprime numbers among 1,2,9,13,42,264. More adequate understanding would be demonstrated if the student could state the principle defining why some were prime (i.e., what common characteristic they possessed).

A *principle* is a statement which relates two or more concepts. Other terms commonly used for principle are rule, generalization, conclusion, and definition. Examples of a principle are:

> "Two fractions can be added by finding their lowest common denominator, then multiplying each numerator by the quotient of their original denominator and the lowest common denominator, adding the resulting products, and dividing by their lowest common denominator."
> "Water is a liquid compound composed of hydrogen and oxygen."
> "Certain types of poetic meter are used to heighten tension."
> "Territorial aggrandizement has been a major cause of war."
> "The volume of a gas is a function of temperature and pressure."

Each of the above statements relates two or more concepts in some way. Evidence that a student has learned a principle could be the ability of the student to restate the principle, perhaps in his own words, and to apply the principle to some situation or problem. However, simply repeating the principle is not sufficient evidence for adequate understanding, since to do this the student need only have memorized the appropriate verbal sequence.

The levels of performance for teaching concepts and principles are specified on the evaluation and feedback guide.

TWO STRATEGIES FOR TEACHING CONCEPTS AND PRINCIPLES

The description below emphasizes the basic difference between expository and discovery strategies. Subsequent to this the similarities of the two approaches will be presented.

Expository Strategy

Most expository strategies are a variation of the following sequence. Initially the teacher states the principle or explains the defining characteristics or attributes of the concept. Next, examples of the concept are presented, or in the case of a principle, problems or situations illustrating the principle are given. Finally, students are asked to discriminate examples of the concept from nonexamples, or to apply the principle to some problems or situations.

For example, if you were to teach the concept "reptile," you would present the dominant characteristics[1] of the concept (vertebrate, breathes air, scales or plates, etc.). Then, or at the same time, examples of the concept would be presented (e.g., picture of turtle, snake, etc.). Students (or the teacher) would tell why the example belonged to the concept "reptile" by verifying that it possessed the appropriate characteristics. Finally, positive and negative examples would be presented (lizard, fish) and identified as either being or not being examples of the concept "reptile."

As an expository strategy for teaching a principle, consider the generalization, "If communication between two cultures increases, the cultures tend to become more similar." The expository strategy would consist of stating the principle and then presenting examples of its occurrence. Next, the students could be given other examples and asked to determine if the principle held for these. Of course, students could also be asked to generate their own examples and to consider under what conditions the principle might not be valid. But the basic idea in the expository strategy is that the teacher presents the principle.

Discovery Strategy

In the discovery strategy the emphasis is on the student's defining the concept or stating the principle. The teacher's role is to present examples in such a way that

---

[1]The number and complexity of these characteristics would depend on student readiness, long range objectives, and available time.

CONCEPTS AND PRINCIPLES: TEACHING EVALUATION AND FEEDBACK GUIDE

TEACHER'S NAME _____ RATER'S NAME _____ DATE_____

EVALUATION CRITERIA	COMMENTS
1. Excellent understanding. Certain that the concept or principle could be applied in many situations. Stated (or could state) the principle in my own words, or give new examples of the concept. Solved a problem or analyzed a situation utilizing the principle or concept.	
2. Good understanding. As above, but not so certain I could apply the concept or principle to many situations.	
3. Acceptable understanding. Could probably apply the concept or principle to some situations. I had (or would have) some difficulty restating it in my own terms; tried to apply or restate, but was not completely successful.	
4. Serious weakness. Some understanding, some confusion. Doubt if I could restate or apply. Not sure how well I grasp meaning, although I understand the idea in the context in which it was presented.	
5. Vague attention to task. Poor understanding. I know a little more than when I began, but I am sure I do not get the idea. I am uncertain about how or when the concept or principle would be used.	
6. No attention to task. Very poor understanding. Very confused. Could not restate the principle or cite other instances of the concept. I was (or would be) unable to define the concept or apply the principle.	

BASIC TEACHING TASKS

I.	Determining Readiness	1 2 3 4 5 6
II.	Clarifying Objectives	1 2 3 4 5 6
III.	Motivating	1 2 3 4 5 6
IV.	Evalutating	1 2 3 4 5 6

LEARNING TASKS

I.	Concepts and Principles	1 2 3 4 5 6

the student can determine the attributes that are characteristic of the concept or to provide examples or situations from which the explaining principle can be discovered.

When you use this strategy to teach a concept or principle, you first present the examples and ask students to discover the basic characteristic(s) present (or absent) in all of them. Or you can present two groups—examples and nonexamples—of the concept and ask students to tell what characteristic(s) distinguish one group from the other. In the case of a principle, you would present situations or problems and ask students to discover the explanatory principle. This strategy will also require guidance from the teacher in order to conserve time and keep students headed in the right direction. After the defining attributes (labeled by you with the appropriate concept's name) or the relevant principle has been discovered by the students, the concept or principle is verified with additional examples or problems.

If you wanted to teach the concept "reptile" using a discovery strategy, you would present examples of reptiles and ask your students to find similarities. Or you would present examples of reptiles and nonreptiles and ask your students what attributes differentiated the two sets. Then you would label things having those attributes as "reptiles" and present more examples to verify their learning. Guidance would be provided by the type of examples you initially select, their order of presentation, and the questions and cues you use to help students focus on the correct attributes.

Suppose you wanted to teach the principle presented earlier—"If communication between two cultures increases, the cultures tend to become more similar"—using a discovery strategy. In this case you would present examples from which this inference could be drawn and ask students to discover "what occurs when communication increases." When the principle is discovered, the students would be asked to verify it with other examples or perhaps to discover conditions under which it might not be a valid generalization.

The basic difference then between expository and discovery strategies rests in the latter's emphasis on the students' discovering, rather than the teacher's explaining, the defining attributes or explaining principle.

THE BASIC TEACHING TASKS

Whether you use expository or discovery strategies or a combination of the two, the basic teaching tasks will be relevant to the learning of concepts and principles. Therefore, it may be helpful to review the chapters dealing with these tasks. In addition, the following descriptions may help you generate strategies appropriate to your lesson.

Determining Readiness

If students are to identify attributes of a concept, then an important aspect of their readiness will be their understanding of those attributes. For example, if "vertebrate" is to be used as one of the defining attributes of "reptile," then you will want to determine whether students understand *that* concept before using it. If they do not, then it must be taught or a substitute concept must be used (like "backbone"). For principles, an understanding of those concepts and subordinate principles, if any, that are used in the formulation is required. For example, in order to learn the principle, "Charged words can be used to bias a reader's attitude toward a controversial subject," students must have an understanding of several concepts (e.g., "charged words," "attitude"). Before beginning the instruction of this principle then, the students' understanding of these concepts needs to be determined. Likewise, before teaching students to graph systems of linear equations, you would need to know, for example, the adequacy of student understanding or equations, variables, constants, etc. In other words, before proceeding with instruction, you must analyze the principle or concept for its component parts and determine the readiness of the students on the basis of their understanding of these parts.

Fortunately, concepts and principles are seldom taught in isolation; usually you will have some idea of your students' understanding of many of the requisite concepts. Nevertheless, you should not assume understanding without evidence; the time spent in determining readiness (and providing additional instruction when necessary) is small compared to the subsequent gain in meaningfulness for the students.

Clarifying Objectives

The teacher's function in this stage of instruction is to communicate to the students the type of response expected. In the case of a concept this means identifying common elements in a group of objects and learning the appropriate label. It usually means, in addition, discriminating examples of the concept from nonexamples. If, for instance, the concept of "metaphor" is to be learned, then the student should understand that as a result of the lesson he should be able to identify from a variety of figures of speech those which are metaphors or that he should be able to write several metaphors.

When a principle is to be learned, the students should understand that they are to be able to state the rule, generalization, conclusion, etc., that can be drawn from the examples presented, or to state when the principle may be used appropriately. For example, if a principle for evaluating arithmetic progressions is to be taught, the student should understand that he will be able to state the rule for adding arithmetic progressions or be able to evaluate examples of arithmetic progressions.

Motivating

Both discovery and expository strategies can contribute to motivation. "The act of discovery" is widely recognized as a motivating experience. Likewise, most students can identify teachers who are extremely stimulating in presenting material. The extent to which these strategies increase motivation for learning probably depends more on related conditions than on anything inherent in the strategies themselves.

In teaching concepts and principles the following conditions should enhance motivation regardless of whether expository or discovery strategies are being used.

The closer concepts and principles are to the realm of students' experiences and interests, the greater the probability that students will be motivated to learn them. For example, whereas the concept of "oligarchy" may be rather remote for many students, the related concept of "power structure" may relate to existing experiences and interests. This idea suggests that you may select, when possible, concepts that are close to students' experiences, or that you relate unfamiliar concepts with familiar ones.

The examples which are used to illustrate a concept or principle can also be drawn from the realm of students' experiences and interests. For example, the principle "If communication between two cultures increases, the cultures tend to become more similar," may come alive in terms of the "generation gap."

A third approach to increasing motivation (and learning) of concepts and principles is to illustrate them in reality. The more that concepts and principles can be related to real objects and real experiences, the greater the probability of student interest. For example, many of the concepts that surround "the farm" and "the factory" (e.g., tractor, strip-farming, and harvest; and assembly line, foreman, and automation) can be grounded in reality through visits to these places. During such visits the teacher can direct student attention to all kinds of examples of various concepts, or the teacher may ask questions which challenge students to conceptualize and form principles on their own.

Finally, indicating the usefulness of concepts and principles should enhance motivation for learning them. They can be emphasized (in specific ways depending on the particular concept or principle) as tools for interpreting experiences and solving problems.

Evaluating

For both concepts and principles, learning may be evaluated in a number of ways during instruction:

1. New examples of a concept may be introduced for identification and reasons given for their identification.

2. The students may be asked to generate new examples of the concept.

3. Students may be asked to discriminate examples from nonexamples of the concept.

4. The students can restate the principle.

5. The students can apply the principle to problems or situations different from those in which the principle was originally presented.

Whether an expository or a discovery strategy is used, student learning should be determined, since this will help students verify their own understanding and help you plan supplementary or subsequent instruction.

CONCEPTS AND PRINCIPLES: LESSONS FOR ANALYSIS AND EVALUATION

First Lesson: Expository

LESSON	ANALYSIS
T: We are beginning to look at groups of numbers, not just one at a time, but some series or sequences of numbers. Today we'll just consider a special kind of series of numbers. (Writes some examples of arithmetic progressions on the board, discusses some of their characteristics, and gives reasons for studying them.)	Reasons may provide motivation.
Today you are going to learn how to evaluate one such series of numbers. What I mean by this is that if I give you a series like this (writes: $1 + 2 + \ldots + 9 + 10$), then you should be able to find their sum without just adding up all the numbers. In other words, you should write an expression, a formula, that you can use to get the sum of this series or one like it.	Learning objective is clarified; involves a principle dealing with a particular series of numbers.
(Teacher answers some student questions.)	
All right, now to find the sum of this series of numbers, you can use this formula. (Teacher writes $\frac{n}{2}(n + 1)$ on board, and referring to the board gives the following explanation.	Principle to be learned is stated.
In the formula, n is the last number in the series. So what we are doing is adding the first and last number in the series, and multiplying this sum by the number of pairs we have, n over 2. If the series is from 1 to 10, then 10, the last number in the series, is divided by 2 to get 5, times n plus 1, or 11, and the sum of the series is 5 times 11, or 55. Okay, do these examples now, using the formula.	Principle explained. Example provided to evaluate learning of principle.
(Teacher writes two arithmetic progressions on the board for students to evaluate. Students work examples.)	
S: Will this formula work if the series doesn't begin with one or if there isn't just one between each of the numbers?	Question indicates that student is applying the principle to additional series of numbers, and questioning its generalizability. Shows good comprehension.
T: No, not as I've written it. But we'll take up those examples after we've finished this.	Positive reinforcement might be appropriate here.

LESSON	ANALYSIS
(Teacher checks some students' work to evaluate if they have correctly applied the formula.)	If all students are not checked, a question to the class asking if anyone had not computed the correct answer would be in order.

T: All right, you're using the formula properly. Now, let's see if we can figure out why it works. Take this series from 1 to 10. The first thing to notice is that if you add the first and last number together you get 11. (Draws line from 1 to 10 and writes 11 above it.)
    Then if you add the second number in the series and the second from the last number, you also get 11. (Draws a line from 2 to 9 and writes 11 above it.)
    See, 2 and 9 are 11 also.
    What do you get if you add the third number in the series and the third from the last number?
S: Eleven.
T: Right. (Draws line connecting three and eight.) How about four and seven?
S: Eleven. And five and six is eleven too.
	Teacher presents analysis of why principle works.

T: Good. So we have five pairs of numbers, and each pair adds up to eleven. That means that the sum of this series of numbers is 5 times 11, or 55. Now, if we call the last number in the series as n, we can write the sum of this series as n over 2, times $n + 1$. (Writes $\frac{n}{2}(n + 1)$ on board.)	Further analysis of the principle is presented.
In other words, $n + 1$ is the sum of each pair of numbers and n over 2 is the number of pairs. Okay. Try the series from 1 to 20, and let's see why the formula works for this series also. (Writes $1 + 2 + 3 + \ldots + 18 + 19 + 20$ on board.)	A new learning trial is provided. Students and teacher can determine whether learning has occurred.

Second Lesson: Discovery

T: We are beginning to look at groups of numbers, not just one at a time, but some series or sequences of numbers. Today we'll just consider a special kind of series of numbers. (Writes some examples of arithmetic progressions on the board. Discusses some of their characteristics and gives reasons for studying about them.)	Reasons may provide motivation.

LESSON	ANALYSIS
Today you are going to learn how to evaluate one such series of numbers. What I mean by this is that if I give you a series like this.(Writes $1 + 2 + \ldots + 9 + 10$), then you should be able to find their sum without just adding all the numbers up. In other words, you should write an expression, a formula, that you can use to get the sum of this series or one like it.	Learning objective is clarified—involves a principle dealing with a particular series of numbers.
(Teacher answers some student questions.)	
Okay. What you need to do now is to figure out how to write a formula that will give you the sum of this series of numbers. (Points at series $1 + 2 + \ldots + 10$.) You'll need some scratch paper to work on. (Students get paper out.)	
I'll give you a hint to get started. Try arranging numbers in groups. Yes, Darryl?	Approach to learning the principle is stated—students are to discover the principle for themselves.
S: What are we supposed to do again?	
T: Find a formula or a procedure that you can use to find the sum of that series of numbers. In other words, don't just add the numbers up, one plus two plus three and so on. Get a rule or procedure or formula that you can use to find the sum. Remember, try to group numbers together. (Teacher moves around room observing students' work.)	Task clarified. Hint provided.
	Observation should provide important information.
Okay. Several of you have grouped the numbers in pairs, putting the first two together, and the next two and so on. (Writes $(1 + 2) + (3 + 4) + (5 + 6) + (7 + 8) +$ $3 \quad + \quad 7 \quad + \quad 11 \quad + \quad 15 \quad +$ $(9 + 10)$ on board.) 19	Are students lost? Or are they working appropriately on the task?
T: That is a very interesting result, since the difference between the numbers is now four instead of one, and you have a new series of numbers. But that doesn't seem to have led you anywhere. Why don't you try grouping the first and last numbers in the series together and see what happens? When you think you're on to something, raise your hand and we'll check it out. (Teacher moves around the room while students work. Several students raise their hands and teacher checks with them.)	Teacher reinforces students' efforts.
	Additional hint provided. Possibly too much help too soon.

LESSON	ANALYSIS
Okay. Some of you found that if you group the first and last numbers you always get 11. (Teacher writes: 1 + 2 + 3 + 4 + 5 + 6 + 7 + 8 + 9 + 10 	This example provides considerable assistance. Possibly teacher should let students make this step.
See if you can use that to find the sum of the series. Raise your hand when you do. (Several hands go up immediately. Teacher interacts with these students. Eventually, many hands have gone up.)	
All right. You found that there are 5 pairs of 11, so the sum of that series is 5 times 11, or 55. Suppose we call the last number in the series "n" Now write a formula for the sum of this article. (Teacher observes a few students.)	Excellent development of the principle. Is teacher attending only to rapid learners? Possibly some hints could be given only to students having difficulties.
Okay. You got $n + 1$, which is the 11 part, and now you need to get an expression for the number of pairs.	
S: n over 2.	
T: Why is that?	
S: You have 10 numbers, so there are 5 pairs and n over 2 is 5.	
T: That's right. So the formula is n over 2 times n plus 1.	
S: Will that work if the series doesn't begin with one, or is it different like the other series?	Student thinking of new examples. Indicates good comprehension.
T: It might not. We'd better check that out. First though, let's work out one more example and make sure we've all got the idea straight.	

CONCEPTS AND PRINCIPLES: SUGGESTED ACTIVITIES

1. Before teaching your lesson, consider using both an expository and a discovery strategy for the same learning objective. Practice both strategies with a friend. A variation of this activity is to evaluate two similar demonstrations (expository and discovery) in class and try to determine which will be more effective.

2. With two groups of students or colleagues, teach the same concept or principle using both strategies. Obtain ratings of their interest in the two lessons, time the length of the lessons, and assess learning (perhaps with a short quiz). Any differences?

3. Deciding what to teach in the lab can be a problem. Examine textbooks used in elementary or secondary subjects and describe at least ten key concepts and principles that are taught in a grade level for which you might be responsible. Then examine textbooks for the same subject, but for a later or earlier grade and determine whether these concepts and principles are also considered, and if so, how the treatment differs.

4. You may wish to work with others in teaching the lesson. Teams may consist of two or more members, the upper limit being decided only by appropriateness of the combinations. Good combinations can be made among many teaching fields. We have found outstanding lessons originating from a variety of combinations: for example, science, social studies, and English; music, foreign language, and home economics; and physical education and art.

You should use the team to accomplish what you cannot accomplish alone. To do this, your team will have to assess carefully the interests and abilities of the different team members. Some team members may be best at presenting information, while others can do best in leading a discussion. Still others might work best on a one-to-one basis, i.e., working individually with pupils who are either ahead or behind most members of the class.

Team teaching also provides the possibility for teacher interaction (e.g., teachers disputing one another before the class) and for role-playing (e.g., where one teacher plays the role of a proponent of a point of view and another teacher takes a stand against it). Team teaching should facilitate flexibility in how you organize your pupils: for example, organizing the pupils in large groups, small discussion groups, and working with individuals.

Although spontaneous teacher interaction during the lesson may become one of the most exciting aspects of team teaching, for this lesson we stress the importance of careful planning. A large factor in its success or failure will be the thoroughness of preparation.

5. References:

For two of the best descriptions of "discovery" and "expository" strategies see "The Act of Discovery" by Jerome S. Bruner, *Harvard Educational Review,* Winter, 1961, pp. 21-32; and "Reception versus Discovery Learning in Classroom Instruction" by David P. Ausubel, *Educational Theory,* January

1961, pp. 21-24. (Both of the above articles are also reprinted in *The New Social Studies in Secondary Schools: An Inductive Approach* by Edwin Fenton, New York: Holt, Rinehart and Winston, Inc., 1966.)

chapter 8

Problem-Solving

Problem-solving has many definitions. For this laboratory lesson we prefer not to approach this task narrowly but to give you wide latitude in generating your lesson. Minimum conditions for problem-solving require more than recall of information and involve a question or questions which, at the beginning of instruction, are unresolved or possibly not even formulated by your students.

Beyond these minimum conditions the following descriptions of alternate approaches to problem-solving may help you generate a meaningful lesson within your teaching field. You might consider what is known and unknown about a problem: for example, (1) How well formulated is the problem? (2) Have methods of solving the problem been generated? (3) Is a solution to the problem known? Relative to these three questions is the question, To whom are these aspects of a problem known? To experts in the field? To the teacher? To beginning students?

Another way to think about problem-solving is to consider the different kinds of problems existing in special fields, such as home economics, mathematics, science, social science, history, art, etc. The problems and methods of solution in some of these fields are fundamentally different from one another, and you will want to consider how experts formulate and solve their particular problems.

Problem-solving has been conceptualized as consisting of divergent problems (more than one acceptable answer) and convergent problems (only one correct answer). Often teachers are accused of dealing only with convergent problems—or making convergent problems out of divergent ones—with problem-solving degenerating into a guessing game in which the students try to determine what answer the teacher wants. Of course both convergent and divergent problems can result in this kind of guessing game, although either type of problem can stimulate independent thinking.

Building on your previous laboratory lesson dealing with concepts and principles, you may also view the task of problem-solving as the application of known concepts or principles to an unresolved situation or to an unanswered question. Application of a concept or concepts to a new situation may result in a more specific concept or the generation of a new principle. Applying a principle to a new situation may result in alteration of the principle or possibly a higher-order principle.

Given your teaching field and your experiences, you may be able to generate an additional approach to problem-solving or to combine and/or elaborate one of the approaches thus far described. To further clarify and extend your alternatives in this lab lesson, we will discuss the nature of two problem situations which are fundamentally different in terms of what is known about the formulation of the problem.

In the first problem situation, nothing is known about the problem because it has not been formulated. Whether methods of solution or specific solutions are known is dependent on what problems are formulated. The teacher and/or students will identify a broad area or possibly focus on some specific data or phenomena, and the "problem-solving" will consist of formulating questions about the phenomena. For example, a social studies teacher may focus on the behavior of people under stress; a science teacher may have students observe the hatching of chicks; and an art teacher may ask students to "contemplate" a mass of unmolded clay. In each case the emphasis is on raising questions about the phenomena involved—on asking good questions rather than finding correct answers.

The second problem situation consists of a well-formulated problem. The extent of available methods for solving the problem and known solutions will vary. The teacher presents the problem as clearly as possible, and then either guides the students toward the solution or solutions, or presents the solution to the problem. For example, a mathematics teacher might ask students to determine the formula for finding the area of a parallelogram after they have learned to find the area of a square; a history teacher might ask students to seek out the reasons for the passage of a particular law given certain related documents; a science teacher might have students determine the effect of a vitamin supplement to the diet of gerbils; and an art teacher might challenge students to combine paint and clay in expressing certain kinds of feelings.

The emphasis here is on appropriate application of concepts and principles to achieve defendable solutions to problems. Formulations of problems and solutions of problems for these two situations are illustrated in the two demonstration lessons at the end of this chapter.

You may have to generate your own criteria for levels of performance depending on the kind of problem-solving lesson you teach. However, the evaluation and feedback guide on page 115 may be helpful in gaining feedback about your lesson.

PROBLEM-SOLVING STRATEGIES

Discovery and Expository

Both discovery and expository approaches are used for problem-solving. (You may wish to review the discussion of these strategies in the preceding chapter.) In using a discovery strategy, your objective is to guide students in formulating and solving a problem. With expository strategies, you generate and solve the problem yourself and then ask your students to repeat these behaviors for a similar (but not the same) problem. The two strategies merge, containing elements of both, when (a) the teacher, in the discovery strategy, specifies exactly which concepts and principles are relevant for the problem's situation; or (b) in the expository strategy, the "similar problem" to which the students are to apply the teacher's method of solution differs sufficiently from the original problem to require new concepts or principles in arriving at a solution. Elements of both an expository and discovery approach will be present in each of the remaining problem-solving strategies.

Problem Structuring

"What would happen if . . .?" is the basic format for problem structuring. You ask students to consider alternatives or to discard assumptions or to look at a new situation and formulate reasonable consequences. A demonstration, experiment, or verbal description may be used to structure the problem, leaving to the students the task of inferring consequences. For instance, "Suppose Shakespeare really didn't write that play. Would it make any difference? Why or why not?" "Let's assume that the shortest distance between two points isn't a straight line . . . ." "What do you suppose will happen if you mix those compounds together . . . ?"

What happens next in using problem structuring strategies depends on your objectives. You may want as many consequences as your students can generate, without regard to whether they use previously covered concepts and principles. Or, probably more typically, you want particular concepts and principles applied to the problem. In that case, you will provide considerably more guidance to the students' exploration of consequences. Your objective may not require any particular consequences, but rather a specific methodology. For example, given a particular problem, consider what conclusions result from applying this methodology: (1) define the problem, (2) form hypotheses, (3) gather evidence to test the hypotheses, (4) form tentative conclusions. In this case, what the student must solve is how to apply the methodology to the immediate problem. In other words, "What happens when you try applying this procedure to the problem at hand?"

Utilizing Groups

Because of the complexity of many problems and the social context in which they must be solved, and because problem-solving is increasingly accomplished

PROBLEM-SOLVING: TEACHING EVALUATION AND FEEDBACK GUIDE

TEACHER'S NAME _____ RATER'S NAME _____ DATE _____

EVALUATION CRITERIA	COMMENTS
II. Problem-Solving	
1. Excellent. I was able to formulate or solve a problem (or, given time, could make considerable progress in achieving these ends.) I would feel confident in continuing work on this problem or in attempting similar problems.	
2. Good. I formulated or solved a problem, but I feel uncertain about my ability to continue working on this or similar problems.	
3. Acceptable. Some progress made in formulating or solving a problem, but I am uncertain about aspects of the problem.	
4. Serious weakness. Some aspect of the problem is completely unclear.	
5. Vague attention to task. Poor understanding. I am unclear about the nature of the problem-solving task.	
6. No attention to task. I am very confused. I don't believe the lesson had anything to with problem-solving.	

BASIC TEACHING TASKS

I.	Determining Readiness	1 2 3 4 5 6
II.	Clarifying Objectives	1 2 3 4 5 6
III.	Motivating	1 2 3 4 5 6
IV.	Evaluating	1 2 3 4 5 6

LEARNING TASKS

I.	Concepts and Principles	1 2 3 4 5 6
II.	Problem-Solving	1 2 3 4 5 6

115

by teams of people with differing competencies, using groups of students to work on problem-solving will often be appropriate. The nature of the groups, their degree of structure, the differentiation of individual contributions within the group, and the expected outcomes will depend on the specific problem involved. The possibility of independent study in conjunction with the use of groups should not be overlooked either. For example, once the group members decide which aspects of the problem could best be handled individually, rather than collectively, students could select aspects on the basis of interest or special competence and pursue them independently.

If you use this strategy in the lab, where time may be limited, a useful focus might be simply the group's deciding which sources of information or which questions are most important or, if these are clear, determining whose responsibility various parts of the problem might be.

Brainstorming

Brainstorming may be a good strategy to use when a problem has no obviously correct solution, when the problem itself is not well-defined, or when there are many unspecified conditions that may affect the method and solution of the problem. This means allowing periods of time when students contribute any idea which comes to mind about a given problem, without evaluation or corrective feedback. The focus could include possible solutions, methods of solution, or simply questions or ideas about the problem.

Brainstorming is a useful strategy for stimulating involvement in the problem and for getting original, though often poorly formulated, ideas into the open. It will often be followed by evaluative sessions in which the emphasis is on selecting and extending good ideas that have come from the session, rather than criticizing every suggestion.

Of course, you cannot use all of these strategies in a single lab lesson. You will want to determine carefully the nature of the problem you wish to deal with and then think through a few strategies (or possibly alternate strategies) which you can test out in attempting to encourage this complex behavior.

BASIC TEACHING TASKS

Regardless of which of the preceding strategies you select, the basic teaching tasks continue to be relevant for problem-solving.

Determining Readiness

Student interest in the problem should be assessed. If you feel sufficient interest is lacking, it will be necessary to generate this student interest, or you may wish to select an entirely new problem. Whether you determine this aspect of readiness prior to instruction or during instruction will depend on how well you know your students and on what you know about them. Observations of their behavior in earlier problem-solving situations, content and activities that generally have interested and seemed important to them, papers, test performance, self-reports, and other expressions of interest will all provide information useful in selecting problems and teaching strategies. Whatever problem you are dealing with, it will be useful to analyze the various concepts, principles, and skills related to the problem. You may find that students are unable to solve a problem because they lack some of these important related learnings.

Clarifying Objectives

Problem-solving is difficult enough without the additional confusion generated by vaguely stated expectations. Students need to know what is expected of them in problem-solving—whether raising questions or finding answers is important, what kinds of conditions are imposed on their explorations, and what a "question" or "solution" entails. The objective should be stated and clarified as soon as possible during instruction.

Motivation

Motivation, particularly long-term motivation, is extremely important in problem-solving. Many of the strategies discussed in the chapter on motivating will be appropriate. In addition, there may be increased motivation as a result of the students' successfully solving a problem or generating an interesting question. The expectations of obtaining a solution to a problem and its actual accomplishment will often be very rewarding. The motivation for grappling with problems that are important to the student (even when the problem is extremely difficult or the answer unknown) should not be overlooked, particularly when you are dealing with students of high ability and creativity.

Evaluation

Evaluating will range from determining whether a student has arrived at a specific answer to a problem to the judgment of complex products (essays, methods, data, apparatus, pictures, diagrams, etc.). Establishing criteria for self-evaluation will be important, particularly with regard to divergent, unknown, and value-laden problems. Feedback in the form of guidance, judgments about progress, and support in attempting to solve problems will be important factors in helping students determine whether they are proceeding in appropriate directions. Regardless of the type of problem, confirmation or discussion of the students' efforts and solutions should be provided.

PROBLEM-SOLVING: LESSONS FOR ANALYSIS AND EVALUATION
Lesson A

LESSON	ANALYSIS
T: I notice that most of you have been spending a lot of time looking at the ant farm that Don brought to class yesterday, and you seem very interested in it. I wonder if today we might talk for awhile about the ant farm and maybe see if there are some things that you would like to learn about ants. What interests you most about the ants? What kinds of questions do you have about what Don's ants are like or what they do?	Lesson is built upon student interest.
S: I want to know how many there are in there.	Questioning emphasized.
S: Yeah. And what kinds of ants are they?	
S: Red!	
T: Okay, I can see that we're going to need someone to write down the questions. Anyone? (two students volunteer.) Let's write the questions on the board. Now we'll have a record of the questions. When we're finished, you can decide what questions you'd like to work on. What we'll do now is just get all the questions we can think of that interest us.	Importance of students' questions is recognized through this activity. Also aids the exploration by providing visual record—eliminates necessity to recall.
	Shows that activity will have future significance. Indicates lesson objective. However, "to work on" is not too clear.
S: What do they eat?	
S: Dirt. (laughter)	
T: That is a very good question. I wonder what they do eat.	
S: What do they do with the dead ants?	
S: Do they fight?	
S: Do they bite?	
S: Haven't you ever had an ant bite your leg?	
T: Good question, Janice. Good answer Tommy. But we don't know for sure if Don's ants are the kind that bite, do we? What other questions do we have?	
S: I wonder if ants can think?	Students seem primarily interested in factual information. Reasons and implications could be built on these facts later. (Should the teacher try to direct them to more significant questions at this point?)
S: Do they always live in the ground?	
S: How long does it take for the eggs to hatch?	
S: Which one is the queen? (Questioning continues for several minutes.)	

LESSON	ANALYSIS
T: You've asked a lot of interesting questions as we can see by looking at all of them on the board. Now, how can we answer these?	Mainly brainstorming to this point, with considerable teacher support for questioning. Lesson now directed toward answering questions.
S: I know the one that's the queen.	Teacher's questions are misinterpreted.
T: How do you know?	
S: It's the big one.	
T: Is the queen always the biggest? I didn't know that.	
S: Is there a king? (laughter)	
T: That could be very important to know. How would you find out if there is? Okay, these are questions that we can answer. But how can we? What will we have to do to answer them? John?	Teacher refocuses discussion. Good use of questions. (Visual record now becomes especially important.) Many questions should be clarified by this activity, e.g., What will be accepted as evidence that ants "think"?
S: We can watch the ants and see.	
T: That's certainly one very good way. Let's go down the list and see which questions we can answer by watching some ants—and we'll see if there are some questions we don't think we can answer that way. . . .	Apparently several ways to answer questions will be explored in the lesson.

Lesson B

T: What do you call these diagrams on the board and these things suspended from this frame? (12 inch by 24 inch wooden frame with small weights and pulleys) Steve?	Prior knowledge assessed, but only from one student.

Diagram

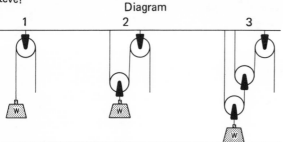

S: Pulleys.

LESSON	ANALYSIS
T: All right. Good. These are systems of pulleys. This one wheel is a pulley, that is a wheel over which you can pass a rope, and believe it or not, do what we shall call work.	
Jamie, do you think you'll ever need to know how to use a pulley?	Interest assessed—little information gained.
S: Well, (laughter) . . . No.	
T: You're probably right, but I think you'll find this interesting, and I'll give you a chance to work with these pulleys and try to figure some things out. If you girls want to be able to tell your boyfriend how much muscle it will take to lift the engine out of his car, you will soon find out.	Problem related to a concrete situation.
I want you to get three things out of this lesson. I want you to be able to explain to me what mechanical advantage means. I want you to be able to tell me what the mechanical advantage is for each of these three systems of pulleys (pointing to the board). And finally I want you to figure out the principle for finding the mechanical advantage of these pulley systems and any pulley system. Okay, who can tell me what mechanical advantage means?	Objectives stated. Extended objectives. Assumes students can remember them, and also understand "mechanical advantage." Several problems have been stated.
S: That means the amount of force you have to apply to move or lift something—well, I mean the ratio of the force you apply to the weight you move. For example, if you use 10 pounds of force to move 50 pounds, you have a mechanical advantage of 5.	
T: Right. Linda, did you get that? Can you explain it?	
S: No, I really don't get it.	
T: Well, as I develop an example, we'll come back to it, and make sure you do understand it. Okay, here's our first pulley system—just one pulley. How much force applied to this end do you think it will take to lift this weight? (Steve raises his hand.) Steve, you seem to know this material really well. I'd like you to start working on number three—see if you can figure the mechanical advantage of that one.	Wide divergence of comprehension indicated by two students. Attempt made to involve Steve in a more difficult problem.
T: Jim, do you know or can you take a guess?	
S: Well, I guess it would take the same amount of weight—the pulley only changes the direction—you have to pull instead of lift.	Problem-solving is conducted through interaction and experimentation with the minature pulley system.

T: Very good, and if that is true this will be a mechanical advantage of one—that is it takes the same amount of force for the weight you lift or the work you do.

Jamie and Linda, can you check Jim out on this—go ahead and use these weights—and see if what he says is true.

Two students involved in activity.

T: Steve, let me see what you have for number three? Great, I thought that might trip you up. Would you work with Jamie and Linda and help them check these out—now mostly watch, don't help too much.

Steve involved in another way. His knowledge used to help other students.

S: Which of the weights should we use?

T: Use any you wish.

S: Okay, he's right. They hold each other up.

T: Do you agree, Linda? Maybe it's just the friction of the pulleys?

S: No, it pulls this little one down. But these balance each other.

T: All right, let's go to the second diagram. . . . (Lesson continues in this manner with other students being drawn in for examples and to check out the answers on the real pulley system. Steve stays involved working with students on the pulley system.)

T: Well, we're doing great, but now listen carefully and see if you can solve this problem. So far we've figured out that the mechanical advantage of diagram #1 is one and diagram #2 is two. And we've had two suggestions about the principle involved—that it's one less than the number of ropes, or that it is the number of pulleys being used. Well, you may think that the mechanical advantage of #3 is three, but notice that it has three pulleys and five ropes. One or both of our principles must be wrong.

Dissonant situation created from students' own answers. This is a new problem which demands the generation of a new principle.

We'll end for now, but by tomorrow see if you have this problem figured out—that is, try to find what the mechanical advantage is, and tell me the principle for determining mechanical advantage.

PROBLEM-SOLVING: SUGGESTED ACTIVITIES

1. For discussion: What are the key problems and the methods used to solve problems in the subject(s) that you teach? To what extent do textbooks in various grade levels emphasize problem-solving?

2. For discussion: To what extent was problem formulation as compared to problem solution emphasized in the laboratory lessons of your teaching group? Did these emphases seem to differ with respect to subject area? Are there more apparent differences when students are relatively knowledgeable in the content than when their understanding is more rudimentary?

3. One way to think of laboratory teaching (and, of course, classroom teaching) is as a very complex problem-solving situation. To begin with, the problem isn't even very well formulated. "To help students learn" is not clear at all. Learn what? "To help?" (Help!) A course syllabus is an aid, but usually objectives are not clearly stated ("2/3 of the year should be spent on grammar and syntax, the remaining 1/3 on literature"!). In the lab, the problem is perhaps even more difficult, since you have no guidelines for appropriate content.

Once you have formulated an idea of what to teach, you must decide how to teach (i.e., what strategy to use). Then you need to determine, using your observations and feedback, the adequacy of your solution. But even this is difficult to do, since you may have (and there are) multiple criteria for success. For example: Did students attain the objective? Were they interested in the lesson? Were ratings sufficiently high? Did the instructor think it was a good lesson? Did I enjoy teaching it?

Listed below are a number of reasons for selecting a teaching strategy. Each of these may have played some part in your choice of strategies for your problem-solving lesson. Rank these from one (most important) to seven (least important) in their order to importance in your decisions about how to teach.

Students will be interested in the lesson.

I will enjoy teaching the lesson.

Students will learn best with this strategy.

I just want to try it out and see what happens.

I am familiar with the strategy, comfortable with it, and know what to do.

I expect good feedback from instructor or colleagues.

It requires less preparation time.

Other:

Although it might be possible to rank order the above in terms of an "ideal teacher," we would prefer not to think in those terms. Instead, consider each as a reasonable, appropriate rationale for selecting a teaching strategy in a laboratory situation. Then consider the following questions:

a. Would you behave any differently if your rank ordering were inverted? If so, how?

b. Do your reasons for deciding how to teach interfere with *your* learning other strategies? That is, are you so locked in to some particular pattern that you are not considering other alternatives?

c. What are the long range consequences of the reasons which determine how you teach?

d. Have your reasons for selecting teaching strategies changed since you first taught in the lab?

4. References:

For one of the classic works, and still among the most readable and provocative books on problem-solving, see *How We Think,* by John Dewey, Boston: D. C. Heath & Company, 1909, 1933.

Many ideas on problem-solving for elementary school teaching are contained in *Children's Thinking,* by David H. Russell, Boston: Ginn and Company, 1956.

Two of the best analyses of problem-solving (although complex and difficult works) are: *Reflective Thinking: The Method of Education,* by Gordon H. Hullfish and Philip G. Smith, New York: Dodd, Mead & Co., 1961; and *Reliable Knowledge,* by Harold A. Larrabee, Boston: Houghton Mifflin, 1945, 1964.

chapter 9

Attitudes

"It's not that he can't learn; he just doesn't want to."

"She accuses her fellow students of intolerance, yet she can't accept *them* when they express *their* feelings."

"They can do the problems when they have the formula, all right, but if you give them a problem that isn't obvious immediately, they want to know what the formula is."

"Several students in the class are actively working with one of the political parties for the coming election—they are almost fanatical about their favorite candidates."

The above statements reflect different types of attitudes. For this laboratory lesson you will be dealing with attitudes—attempting to *change* students' attitudes in a particular direction or assisting students in *becoming aware of and clarifying* their own and others' attitudes.

An attitude can be defined in many ways: as the degree of interest in some object or idea, as a positive or negative feeling, as the tendency to approach or avoid, as the extent to which one values an object or idea, or as the degree to which an idea or principle implies that there is some object (person, idea, behavior, physical object) toward which a feeling is directed.

It is important to understand that an attitude is inferred from behavior and is a concept used to explain certain constancies of behavior. For example, when you say "John has a very negative attitude toward my class," you are inferring an attitude from behaviors which you have observed. John may not turn in his homework; he may refuse to participate in class or cause problems which interfere with the learning of others; he may be absent from class frequently and forget to bring his book to class when he is in attendance; he may have told you that he feels he is gaining very little from the class.

A second example, involving a different kind of attitude and attitude object, would be "Mary is a fine citizen and shows a strong love of country." One teacher may have made this statement by observing the kinds of statements which Mary is constantly making about the benefits of democracy as opposed to the evils of communism. A second teacher may have made the statement by observing that Mary has run for a school office, keeps well informed on national affairs, and has worked for passage of a local ordinance.

The above examples are intended to show how attitudes are inferred from behaviors. In addition the examples indicate the complexities involved in inferring both attitude objects and types of attitudes. Possibly John's behavior is a result of the particular teacher rather than the content or class as such; perhaps another student in the class greatly influences his behavior; or possibly he works all night and lack of sleep produces his behavior. Possibly Mary has very little knowledge of political and economic systems of the United States or of major communist countries. Her involvement in school and local politics could be a result of pressure from her parents; on her own she might behave differently. In deciding what attitudes and attitude objects to deal with for your laboratory lesson, you must have in mind several behaviors that are relevant to the attitude objects and indicative of different types of attitudes (many of these behaviors for your laboratory lesson will be verbal).

Whether you are setting out to *change* or *clarify* attitudes depends to some extent on the kinds of attitudes and attitude objects implicit in your lesson, but this is ultimately a philosophical decision which you will need to make. Generally we feel the teacher is responsible for developing (changing) student attitudes which will facilitate, rather than impede, successful learning; however, it is the teacher's responsibility only to probe (clarify) student attitudes which involve controversial objects such as capitalism, socialism, communism, urbanization, and "the good life." Said in another way, we believe that you should attempt to develop positive attitudes toward learning, but that the student has the right to develop his own attitudes toward what is learned.

If this distinction appears a simple one, you will begin to see how complex it is when you start to think through how you will approach specific kinds of attitudes and attitude objects. In the first place, good arguments can be made against having teachers teach any kind of attitude. For example, if the student understands the consequences of his negative attitude toward a subject, it might be his right to maintain that attitude without interference from a teacher. On the other hand, good arguments can be made for direct influence of all kinds of attitudes—one basis for this being an assumed student immaturity or the necessity of influencing the development of character. And in between learning and controversial attitude objects are such objects as science, history, self, rationality, human beings, freedom, and order which relate to both learning and substance. It may be appropriate to attempt to influence directionally and at the same time to probe for independent attitude formation with respect to these objects.

Your task for this lesson then is to select an attitude object (idea, person, etc.) toward which you wish to influence attitudes and to decide what kind of influence (change or clarification) will be used.

The observation form which follows should be used in evaluating and gaining feedback on your attitude lesson.

EVALUATION CRITERIA	COMMENTS
III. Attitudes	

1. Excellent. No real weaknesses. Attitudes were changed or clarified in a significant way. I gained new awareness or new insights into my own or others' attitudes.

2. Good. At least one identifiable weakness. Attitudes were changed or clarified. Some new awareness and insights were stimulated.

3. Acceptable. Several weaknesses. Attitudes may have changed a little or were clarified to some extent but little awareness or insight developed.

4. Serious weakness. Atttitudes were not changed; clarification was superficial. No new awareness or insight stimulated.

5. Vague attention to task. Attitudes seemed somehow involved in the lesson but there was no attempted change or probing for understanding. If anything, attitudes changed in wrong direction.

6. No attention to the task.

BASIC TEACHING TASKS

I.	Determining Readiness	1 2 3 4 5 6
II.	Clarifying Objectives	1 2 3 4 5 6
III.	Motivating	1 2 3 4 5 6
IV.	Evaluating	1 2 3 4 5 6

LEARNING TASKS

I.	Concepts & Principles	1 2 3 4 5 6
II.	Problem-Solving	1 2 3 4 5 6
III.	Attitudes	1 2 3 4 5 6

STRATEGIES FOR CLARIFYING ATTITUDES

The key to clarification of attitudes is to provoke students to explore their own attitudes: to be aware of their attitudes, to clarify the kinds of attitudes and attitude objects involved in their thoughts, to use logic and to seek evidence to support their attitudes, and to be aware of the effects of their attitudes on their own behavior and that of others.

Discussion and presentation strategies can be applied to the exploration of attitudes. Students can be questioned about why they think they have particular attitudes, how they think others' attitudes differ from theirs, what their attitudes cause them to overlook, how well they can support their attitudes, and how their attitudes affect others. Lecturing, particularly based on a case study, will be appropriate in demonstrating how attitudes have affected a person. Also, expository probing of the teacher's own attitudes on a particular subject may provoke students to examine their own attitudes.

Several types of projection strategies—i.e., being someone else—will be useful by allowing students to empathize with the attitudes of others and to explore attitudes and actions which they don't have to defend. For example, in role-playing, a student may try to express the attitudes of a person of another race regarding a specific incident. Or students may play roles which interrelate with one another—for example, in acting out a city council meeting (simulation), in trying to win a majority of supporters in a race relations conflict (gaming), to act out their conceptions of how a family will resolve the problem of a delinquent daughter (socio-drama), or to argue both sides of an issue (debate).

Creating attitude conflicts within or between pupils will enhance the need for clarification and resolution of conflict. For example, a student may say that violent revolution is never justified and then turn around and say that the American Revolution is an exception. Making the student aware of this inconsistency should create an imbalance which will motivate attempts to resolve the conflict. Or in a class discussion one student may confidently state that anyone has the right to wear beards, long hair, and generally to dress as they wish. A second pupil may say with great scorn that long haired men and unkempt women ought to be locked up. Such disagreement opens up the possibility of exploring the attitudes involved within and between the two individuals.

Presentation of extreme attitudes—for example, those of a pacifist and a soldier on a question such as the morality of wiping out a strategic enemy village—may cause one to probe his own attitudes toward the problem.

While many dramatic and intensive strategies seem appropriate in the exploration of attitudes, there are good reasons to consider using "mild" strategies. Because our attitudes are so important to us and because we have usually explored them very little, we are fairly defensive about having them exposed or challenged by others. Thus, nonthreatening strategies may actually open us to self-exploration more than intensive, threatening ones. For example, one probe may be better than two when the second probe makes the student feel he is being backed into a corner. Nonevaluative statements which focus on an attitude but do not demand a response may lead to examination of the attitude—for example, "That's interesting that he makes you get so mad." Also, being a good listener, being open, attempting to empathize, being nonevaluative may provide the provocative sounding board which many students need in order to be able to explore their own attitudes.

Students may also be encouraged to explore their attitudes on a continuing basis by keeping journals or writing a series of papers. For example, a teacher may be interested in conceptions of the "good life," in conservation of plant and animal life, in development of sensitivity to other human beings, or in varieties of expression. By keeping a daily record of perceptions related to the objects of interest, the student should develop a greater awareness of and basis for his attitudes. Over time he may see how his attitudes change in relation to his experience.

STRATEGIES FOR CHANGING ATTITUDES

Experiences

Many attitudes are formed on the basis of little or no direct experience with the attitude object. On occasion, you can provide for such experience directly, through field trips or by bringing the experience directly into the classroom. Often you can supplement the experience with films, recordings, and other instructional materials.

If anxiety or strong avoidance tendencies are characteristic of many of the students' attitudes, then you will want to build gradually toward the experience. For example, the study of reptiles in a science class might include as an objective the handling and inspecting of various species of reptiles. Those of you who fear snakes, lizards, etc., will recognize the problems involved in providing actual experiences with the attitude object. However, we have witnessed a lesson in which the teacher was able within twenty minutes to bring his students to the point of holding a large lizard. The instructor began the lesson (holding the lizard) with a discussion of its characteristics. He moved around the room slowly, letting each student look at it. He asked students to volunteer to touch it and describe how they felt, and finally he asked them to volunteer to hold and inspect it. Most did. The teacher extinguished, at least temporarily, the students' negative (avoidance) attitude by gradually providing experiences that the students could cope with.

In any case, the experiences you provide using the attitude object need to be positive to cause students to be more likely to approach, be more interested in, or value it. In this strategy your emphasis lies in developing an experience which will establish the positive, pleasant, or nonthreatening characteristics of the attitude object.

Providing for Positive Consequences

Whereas the previous strategy, experience, emphasized providing positive conditions for attitude change, providing positive consequences requires that students be reinforced for behavior indicative of a desired attitude. For example, to enhance positive attitudes toward verbal learning in a language class, students can stage short plays or shows using a vocabulary they have acquired, or a native speaker can be brought in so that students understand that they can use what they are learning.

Providing positive consequences is basically a reinforcement strategy. The range of positive reinforcers at your disposal is great: praise, encouragement, high grades, attention, social approval, and allowing increased independence for the student. Where attitude change, and not just clarification, is the desired objective, you should be relatively certain that positive consequences will result from the activity. To do this you will have to be clear about those behaviors which you wish to reinforce. In the laboratory, because of time limitations, your use of this strategy may be restricted to immediate reinforcements or to helping students plan for longer range success which will be reinforcing.

As an example of providing for positive consequences, suppose that one of your attitudinal objectives is that students become aware of the long range dangers of pollution and take some action to alert other students, parents, or the community to these dangers. Your task in order to facilitate this objective is to guide the students toward behaviors that are most likely to be rewarded (i.e., in this case, meet with success). For example, student articles printed in the school paper should provide the possibility of reinforcement (by peers, parents, teachers). Encouraging students to present their information to others will emphasize that what they are doing is important, and helping students with a realistic goal which actually results in some change should be extremely rewarding. While each of these examples may result in negative reinforcement (i.e., opposition), students can be supported in viewing these effects as challenges and possibly gain reinforcement from the conflict.

The Teacher as a Model

The adage, "Show, don't tell," applies here. For a teacher to exhort, persuade, or cajole students to be tolerant of differing opinions, and then to reject offhand an idea that conflicts with his own is preaching what isn't practiced. On the other hand, to be accepting of student ideas, to probe or to seek clarification indicates that such behavior is valued and serves as a model for students. Further, if you establish your credibility, your opinions and suggestions are more likely to be attended to and valued.

To use this strategy in the lab, you might decide on a specific behavior that serves as a referent for an important attitude. Then practice that behavior yourself while teaching, and observe to what extent your students also use it. You might, for instance, show your excitement with students' attempts to explain some experiment to determine whether this in turn generates excitement from students.

Role-Playing and Role Reversal

Discussed earlier as an effective strategy for attitude clarification, role-playing may be used to provide conditions for attitude change.

Content can become far more involving to students when they take on a role in which their understanding of the content must be applied. This involvement (positive attitude) occurs in part because it is the student's behavior that is on the line, before his peers and teacher, and others are responding to it. That is, there is a continuity of behavior of which the student provides an important part, and not simply an answer to a teacher's question.

Students may be assigned roles very dissimilar to their own attitudes and characteristics in an effort to help them "see the other side." Thus, roles of a black militant, moderate, white conservative, liberal, etc. debating a proposed school integration plan may produce additional insight if the roles are given to students whose view point on the issue is likely to be different from the assigned role. The student must, for the first time, defend the other's values.

Although role-playing has been primarily used in the various social studies areas, you may readily see its application in other fields. For instance, one way to handle a situation in which the teacher senses considerable anxiety about tests would be to assign different roles (very upset, pretends he doesn't care, parents expect him to do very well, etc.) and simulate a testing situation. To stimulate greater interest in reading or literature in an English class, students could role-play characters from a story or novel, putting them into a new setting. Students in business education courses can role-play on-the-job problems.

BASIC TEACHING TASKS

The key to generating strategies for determining readiness, clarifying objectives, and evaluating in relation to attitudes is to identify the relevant behaviors in which you are interested. Once these behaviors have been identified, and you know what you are looking for, you can communicate the relevant behaviors to pupils, and you have explicit criteria on which to evaluate progress in the change or clarification of attitudes. Because the behaviors which you are most interested in often occur outside the classroom, you may have to settle for behaviors which you believe reflect the primary activity. For example, voluntarily selecting certain kinds of television programs or engaging in political activity may be reflected through verbal expression of the kinds of television programs preferred and the types of political activities engaged in.

Clarifying attitudinal objectives presents special problems. Clarifying objectives prior to instruction may create barriers to attitude change or exploration. For example, one teacher stated at the beginning of a lesson, "When you have completed this role-playing experience you will understand how it feels to be systematically discriminated against." It might be more effective in this case to engage students in a role-playing activity and then, in the context of exploring the feelings experienced by the students, to clarify the objectives of the experience.

Likewise, motivation for attitude change is a complex task. Little evidence exists that exhortation has any effect on attitude change. Structuring and enhancing positive consequences related to attitude exploration and/or change is probably the most relevant motivational strategy.

You may find that self-evaluation is an important evaluating strategy. Rather than placing external judgments on students' attitude change, you may wish to involve students in assessing their own progress in this area.

In view of the strategies for attitude clarification, strategies for attitude change, and the basic instructional strategies, your task now is to select from among these strategies (or to generate a strategy of your own) and attempt to change or clarify student attitudes.

ATTITUDES: LESSONS FOR ANALYSIS AND EVALUATION
Lesson One

LESSON	ANALYSIS
T: Today we're going to deal with a hypothetical situation. Imagine that you are partners in a boutique in Washington, D.C., which you realize has problems with rioting and a high crime rate. These pictures up here are from different parts of Washington. You see some of the areas are pretty bad off, and some of the people are awfully poor. Then here are some of high society and the fancier parts of town. Remember that in Washington these two sets of circumstances aren't separated so much like Harlem in New York or our east side of town.	Begins with something that involves students. Use of visual aids to clarify situation. Reference to familiar situations.
Okay. So you own a boutique downtown where you sell pretty fancy clothing to people from the wealthier part of town. You have everything from sports clothes to fancy furs. It's kind of a new place, but has become quite popular. You all work in the store and have a big stake in it since it's just beginning to really get rolling.	Personalized by giving students a stake in a situation.
Now, one Saturday morning when you're all in the store checking the stock and getting ready to open—soft music playing and all—a guy rushes in waving a gun around wildly. He demands all your cash. You're behind the counter and have a gun in a drawer, an alarm button you can press with your foot, and a phone right by you. What would you do?	
S: I'm scared of guns. I'd just hand him the money, if I weren't too paralyzed. Actually, I'd probably faint on the spot.	Attitude expressed by girl.
S: I'd do what he said, too, but I'd step on the alarm. If he was acting so crazy with the gun and all, I wouldn't mess with him myself, but I'd get the cops as soon as he left.	More aggressive attitude.
S: I'd check where he ran off to, also.	
T: You'd have the police catch him, right?	
S: Sure.	
T: Then you'd identify him?	
S: Sure.	
T: So he's caught red-handed. Then what happens?	
S: He'll go to jail.	
T: What do you think will happen to him in jail? (Silence)	Attitudes connected with reality.
What will happen to his family while he's in jail? (Silence)	Use of silence.

LESSON	ANALYSIS
Okay, Let's change the situation a little. This time the guy is pretty frantic, but instead of asking for money and threatening your life, he starts grabbing furs off the rack. You can tell he's awfully poor, but he's a big strong guy. Would you do the same thing?	Gradual changing of situation—good technique for forcing clarification of attitudes.
S: Does he still have a gun?	
T: Suppose he doesn't?	
S: Well, then I'd use my gun and stop him. I'd get the cops and all. It's the same thing.	
S: No, I don't think so. I mean, if the guy's poor, maybe he's hungry. Oh, I don't know. But what if you pulled your gun and he didn't stop? Would you shoot the poor guy?	Students allowed to interact to teach one another.
S: You can't just let them steal like that. You have to think of our investment too.	Students clearly trying to deal with consequences.
S: You don't have to kill for it. We have insurance.	
S: If we let someone steal from the place, we'll get a lousy reputation with the customers.	
S: Maybe we could talk to him, give him a job or something. If we get the cops, it will wreck our reputation, too, you know. And if you collect insurance, your rates will go up. You have to settle things as quietly as possible.	
S: Like how?	
S: Well, maybe pull the gun on him until he quieted down. Then talk to him like Susan said. Try to help him. Obviously he's bad enough off so that the law isn't keeping him from stealing. You have to go to the source of the problem.	
S: Man, there are lots of people bad off like that. What if they all steal and don't get punished? You've got to keep order. You don't help by letting him get away with it.	
T: Remember Jerry said he wasn't going to let him get away with it. He said he was going to catch the guy, I suppose take the stuff away, and then try to help him. How else could you help?	Considerable freedom allowed in letting students attempt to clarify their attitudes by interacting with one another.
S: Well, we can't give all of them jobs, you know. How about that?	
S: They should take the guy to jail and then try to help him there. Maybe they could train him and then find him a job.	
S: And they could put his family on relief in the meantime.	

LESSON	ANALYSIS
T: Now you're coming up with some really good ideas. Here are some of the problems we've talked about: breakdown in law and order, property rights as opposed to human rights, punishment as opposed to prevention and help. Tonight, I want you to write a critique on one of these problems. You can just support a stand or you can draw up a situation and apply one or several of the issues to it. Your writing should clarify how you feel about at least one of these. You don't have to take a stand, but you have to state as clearly as possible just what the problem is.	Teacher clarifies things students have dealt with—a good conclusion. Clarification doesn't mean closing issues.
Thursday we're going on a field trip. In the morning we'll go to juvenile hall and in the afternoon to the jail. You'll have a chance to see the punishment-prevention problem in our own penal system. Friday, Sgt. Haggle from the police dept., Mr. Young, probationary officer, and Mr. White, a social worker, will be with us to talk with us about some of the questions and ideas we're developing, so keep such questions in mind.	Direct experiences to be provided—exposure to attitude objects and attitudes of adults.

Lesson Two

T: . . .in this. I've been working on it. . . (Teacher looses voice, on purpose) Uh, then, then, well then, then, then, just, then, I, er, I worked awful hard on this project. This, this is a, this project's about an eraser and a piece of chalk, a piece of chalk. Thank you. (Student laughter)	Teacher begins by role-playing an ineffective project presentation.
T: Okay. All right. Now I want you to think about this presentation, and I want Norman to tell me what kind of grade you gave me on that. What did you give me? S: An *F*. T: You gave me an *F*? What did you give me Sally? S: An *F*. T: You grade pretty hard. What if I turned around and did that to you. Cindy? S: I gave you a *D* because you tried. T: Ah, that's nice. I think so, yeah. Curt? S: I gave you an *A*. I thought it was great. T: Did you? S: Yes.	Teacher opens self to evaluation.

LESSON	ANALYSIS

T: Well, good, I've got someone on my side. How about you, Marcello?
 	
S: A *D.*
 	
T: A *D?* Why?
 	
S: Well . . .
 	
T: You didn't think it was quite bad enough for an *F?*
 	
S: No.
 	
T: I tried hard.
    (Student laughter)
 	
T: Okay. Now let's list some good points on this side. Can you think of even one? (Teacher picks up chalk and writes the points the students make on the board)
 	
S: No.
 	
T: Okay. Mike?
 	
S: At least you showed something.
 	
T: I showed something. Some effort, okay? Now you want to put this down on your paper so you'll have something to look at and remember when you're starting to present your project. Okay. Now, let's put some bad points on this side, and I think you are going to have a few more bad ones than good ones. What's one thing I did very incorrectly? Michelle?
 	
S: You turned around and put your back to the class.
 	
T: Okay. I put my back to audience, like I'm doing right now. (Teacher has back to class as she writes on board. Several additional points are developed.)
 	
    Now that we see what is important to do and not to do in our project presentations, who would like to demonstrate to us how you think we ought to present our projects? Okay. Clydine, you be the first one.
 	
S: Can I be second?
 	
T: Okay. (Teacher goes to back of room and Clydine comes up to present her project.)
 	
    Walk right up there and show us how to demonstrate it well.
 	
S: Well, my project's made out of a little treasure chest and a glass lady; and the lady's wearing some of the clothes like in the olden days—see how long it is, and um, I made the treasure chest out of this little kit—we sent off for the kit, and I made it.
	Variety in evaluations is emphasized. Support indicated for effort.
	
	Teacher shows how criticism can be used. Attempt to establish a critical yet supportive climate.
	
	Freedom given to students for interpreting what is good. Student response indicates that the threat of this activity has been reduced.
	
	Encouragement given to student.

LESSON	ANALYSIS
I covered the box so it would look pretty, and I made it where you can open it. And I brought a little— it's an old tiny purse, the kind that they used to have in the olden days. And it's made out of steel and it's 60, 60 years old.	
T: Would you be willing to pass that around, or do you think you'd better not?	Interest indicated in presentation. Suggestion indirectly provided.
S: The purse?	
T: Yes. They might be interested to see that kind of purse—it is very different from the big baskets that we carry today!	
(Student laughter)	
(Clydine gives the purse to a student and returns to her seat and Alan comes to front of room.)	
T: Thank you. Okay, Alan, you said you wanted to be next. Show us a good presentation now. Clydine started off well, she told us that her project was about, and made a good presentation. What's your project? . . . (Alan presents project. Much interaction is encouraged.)	Reinforcement given to student. A critique here might be in order to follow through with the original structure.
T: Thank you. Now Alan and Clydine did several good things in their projects. They talked loud enough so we could hear them. They included the materials they made it out of, showed us, and described it. Alan used questioning, and you all had to listen carefully. Okay, who'll volunteer to be the next one to show your project?	Variety in evaluation is emphasized. Support indicated for effort, but little corrective feedback. Positive attitudes toward presentation of projects seem to be developing. Might more constructive feedback hinder this?

ATTITUDES: SUGGESTED ACTIVITIES

1. Consider some attitude that you feel is important and that you would attempt to help students clarify or change. Then list as many behaviors as you can that are indicative of that attitude, or of the various meanings it may have. If possible, compare your list of behaviors with someone else's list for the same attitude and note the similarities and differences. If there are substantial differences, are you both actually dealing with the same attitude?

2. Several of the films in the "Critical Moments in Teaching Film Series" (Holt, Rinehart and Winston, Inc., 1968) illustrate problems related to attitude clarification and change. You may wish to view one or more of these: "Less Far Than the Arrow," "I Walk Away in the Rain," and "Walls."

3. If you have not been in a role-playing session before, you might wish to try it out with several colleagues with roles that represent important issues or problems to teachers. Some which you might try are:

   a. AF of T and NEA representatives meeting with teachers who are to decide with which organization they will affiliate.

   b. A parent-teacher conference about a problem a child is having. The parent's role could be played in a variety of ways: hostile, anxious, defensive, over-protective, etc.

   c. A meeting attended by principals, supervisors, teachers, parents, and board members to decide whether the schools should go to a nongraded system.

4. References:

For clarifying the teaching of attitudes, you might want to see R. F. Mager's *Developing Attitude Toward Learning.* Palo Alto, Calif.: Fearon Publishers, 1968.

The following are good books in illustrating techniques for value clarification and change: Louis E. Raths, et. al. *Values and Teaching.* Columbus: Charles E. Merrill Publishing Co., 1966; and F. R. Shaftel, *Role-Playing for Social Values.* Englewood Cliffs, New Jersey: Prentice-Hall, Inc., 1967.

chapter 10

Skills

The focus of this laboratory task is on teaching complex psychomotor skills. Such a skill consists of a sequence of motor activities (behaviors) which are performed in a coordinated, integrated way. Examples of psychomotor skills include hitting a golf ball, typing, sewing, playing a piano, constructing the apparatus for an experiment. As you can see, these skills are very important in some fields, for example, physical education, home economics, creative arts, and vocational education. However, to some extent, every school subject includes some types of psychomotor learning.

All of the tasks described above and most psychomotor behaviors also involve other kinds of behaviors. For instance, playing a piano usually involves a complex of cognitive and attitudinal behaviors as well as the psychomotor behaviors necessary to execute a song. Likewise, no school subject deals exclusively with behaviors which involve psychomotor skills. For example, in physical education, learning the rules for a game involves knowledge of principles, and the application of these principles in a game requires problem-solving. Similarly, deciding what type of stitch to use when knitting or what club to use when making a particular golf shot are problem-solving behaviors, whereas producing the stitch and hitting the golf ball are largely psychomotor skills.

Although the emphasis of this lesson is on motor behavior, you may find it useful to think of the task more broadly in order to include learning objectives in your field which are more appropriate in "skills" than under any of the previous three types of learning objectives—i.e., principles and concepts, problem-solving, and attitudes. For example, the following "skills" probably include behaviors which must be coordinated and integrated: map skills, research skills, reading skills, writing skills, speaking skills, discussion skills, and social skills. The strategies discussed in this chapter will probably be relevant for certain of these objectives which are not clearly motor skills.

SKILLS: EVALUATION AND FEEDBACK GUIDE

TEACHER'S NAME _____ RATER'S NAME _____ DATE _____

CRITERIA	COMMENTS
IV. Skills	
1. Excellent. No real weaknesses. Skill was demonstrated, sufficient practice was provided, and appropriate feedback was given. All students were involved. Most students performed the skill at the desired level of performance or understood the skill well enough to monitor their own performance.	
2. Good. At least one identifiable weakness. Much learning was accomplished in the lesson.	
3. Acceptable. Enough was learned for lesson or subsequent instruction to be meaningful. Some aspect of the skill was not learned. to be meaningful. Some aspect of the skill was not learned.	
4. Serious weakness. Some learning was accomplished and the lesson was generally directed to skill learning, but due to insufficient clarification of the skill to be learned, insufficient practice, or lack of feedback, students made only slight progress in learning the skill.	
5. Vague attention to task. Many weaknesses. Little skill learning was accomplished in the lesson.	
6. No attention to task. No skill learning was accomplished.	

BASIC TEACHING TASKS   (circle one)
I.   Determining Readiness 1 2 3 4 5 6
II.   Clarifying Objectives 1 2 3 4 5 6
III.   Motivating 1 2 3 4 5 6
IV.   Evaluating 1 2 3 4 5 6

LEARNING TASKS   (circle if appropriate)
I.   Concepts & Principles 1 2 3 4 5 6
II.   Problem-solving 1 2 3 4 5 6
III.   Attitudes 1 2 3 4 5 6
IV.   Skills 1 2 3 4 5 6

141

The evaluation and feedback guide on page 141 describes levels of performance for teaching skills. In that these skills are often complex and take considerable time to acquire, you should take these factors into account in evaluating a skill lesson.

STRATEGIES FOR TEACHING SKILLS

Part Strategy

Skills are made up of component behaviors. In the part strategy the student learns the separate behaviors independently before practicing sequencing. For instance, in teaching pole vaulting, you would instruct the student separately in the behaviors: proper hand position on the pole, approaching the bar, planting the pole, etc. Or, in teaching how to type, you would present correct preparation of the typewriter, the position of the hands, finger placement, and stroke as separate behaviors. Not only is instruction separate for the major component behaviors, but practice is also. That is, the student learns the major component skills through separate practice in which he performs each behavior until he is sufficiently proficient to proceed to a new behavior. Practice time required for the parts will of course vary considerably depending on the difficulty and complexity of the behavior.

Use of the part strategy does not preclude an initial demonstration or description of the total sequence of behaviors that make up the skill. In fact this is usually desirable for the purpose of motivation, since the objective of instruction will be clarified.

The instructional sequencing of the major component behaviors of the skill can vary considerably. For example, in aiming toward individualizing instruction, students can practice the component they are most lacking. The instruction can also begin with the terminal behavior and work backward to the initial component behaviors, rather than working from the initial component behaviors and proceeding to the final ones. For example, if you were to teach typing using a part strategy, you could teach appropriate posture, hand position, finger position, and stroke, strating with the stroke and working backward rather than beginning with posture and proceeding to the stroke.

Whole Strategy

In the whole strategy, instruction is directed toward the students' learning the appropriate sequence of component behaviors. That is, rather than providing instruction and practice for each major component behavior of the skill, instruction and practice are directed toward the integrated performance of those behaviors. Although the "whole" is emphasized, students must of course be able to perform the component behaviors. However, instruction and practice focus on performing the whole skill rather than its parts. In other words, practice of the parts occurs during practice of the entire sequence of behaviors rather than separately.

As an example of the whole strategy, consider teaching someone to operate a power drill. Major component behaviors would include inserting the drill into the chuck, bringing the drill to the prepared surface, starting the drill, applying the drill to the started hole, etc. In the whole strategy, the student would perform each of the component behaviors in sequence, whereas in the part strategy, each important component would be practiced separately before being put together.

Your choice of a whole or part strategy should be contingent on the type of skill involved. Skills in which appropriate and well-coordinated sequencing is important but the component behaviors are easily performed will probably be best taught using a whole method, since this procedure emphasizes sequencing. Skills whose component parts require new or unusual behaviors or must be learned in order that the whole skill itself be performed, lend themselves to the part method. We might also mention that when one of the component behaviors is necessary for the sake of safety, a modified approach is suggested. For instance, when students are learning proper use of a piece of machinery, they should learn and demonstrate appropriate use of safety devices before proceeding to the whole skill.

Whether you use a whole or part strategy, or some modification of either, there are many teaching behaviors necessary for teaching skills which are not dependent on the particular approach used. In their totality these are certainly more important than whether you use a part of whole approach.

BASIC TEACHING TASKS

Determining Readiness

Three aspects of a student's readiness are of major importance. The first is the student's ability to perform any of the component parts of the psychomotor skill—that is, any of those behaviors that must be integrated in order to perform the skill. For example, in performing a jump shot in basketball, can the student hold the ball correctly? Can the feet be placed appropriately and the correct balance attained? Can the jumping behavior be performed? Can the ball be released correctly? Whether you approach the learning of a skill as the separate practice of component behaviors or the integrated practice of all behaviors, or a combination of these two approaches, it will be important to determine the degree to which component behaviors of the skill can be performed.

A second aspect of readiness is cognitive in that it involves the extent to which students understand the component parts and their correct sequencing. For example, a student may be physically capable of "tucking his head under" when tumbling forward, but with painful consequences not realize its importance. You obviously don't ask for a demonstration to determine readiness when teaching novice students, particularly when physical harm may result. Your instruction in this case begins with assuming no understanding of the required behavior, or else you determine readiness through questioning—by asking students to verbalize the sequence of behavior necessary to perform the skill.

The third aspect of determining readiness is attitudinal. It will be important to determine the students' interest in learning the skill so that you know the extent to which you need to attend to motivational strategies. Also, anxiety may be an important determinant of the amount of practice provided for a skill or the type and amount of expected public performance.

Clarifying Objectives

Communicating to the student what he is expected to learn is, as usual, an important aspect of instruction. It is relatively easy to specify the objective in terms of intended behavior, since a skill is, by definition, a behavior. Likewise, the conditions under which the behavior is to be performed are often obvious from the nature of the activity. Setting suitable performance criteria is another matter. Ideally, the performance criteria would be established individually, by the instructor and student, and be a function of the students' abilities and goals. However, given the constraints of time and instructing large groups of students, a reasonable procedure might be to establish minimally acceptable criteria along with levels of higher performance.

With rare exceptions the teacher can provide a demonstration of the skill himself or use pictures, movies, or illustrations. This activity serves two functions: it clarifies the objective by demonstrating the appropriate intended behavior, and it can show the pattern of separate behaviors which make up the skill.

In addition you should provide an analysis of the skill, a description of the behaviors that need to be coordinated. Skill analysis is often combined with a demonstration of the skill, and in early stages of instruction, is generally restricted to a few components with other refinements added as proficiency in the skill increases.

Motivating

Many of the strategies described in chapter 5 will also be appropriate to the teaching of skills, but the following points are of particular importance.

1. In establishing performance criteria, the use of individualized standards may be highly motivating. That is, rather than aiming for a goal that is set far too high or too low for the student's ability and the amount of instructional time, work with students to help them establish their own goals. This helps the student establish appropriate expectations for his own performance, since it is a

joint effort by the student and the instructor, who can help him set realistic goals. This does not in any sense preclude a student's exceeding expectations, since various performance levels can be defined, and he can be encouraged to do so.

2. Reducing fear of failure and embarrassment can help a student maximize his attainment. Demonstration of a skill often requires performing before peers and that, as most of us can perhaps vividly recall, can inhibit performance. By not singling out students as negative examples, and by providing support for student effort, not just achievement, you can reduce the anxiety attendant to public performance.

3. Communicating the rationale for learning the skill is an important strategy, especially when a very complex skill, composed of many sub-skills, is being taught. Showing students what learning a particular skill will enable them to do (for example, showing a finished product) will often provide an additional incentive for acquiring the skill.

Evaluating

Two general types of evaluation are important.

1. *From the teacher.* As the student performs the skill, the teacher's evaluation function consists of providing feedback, confirming appropriate behavior, and correcting inappropriate behavior. A longer term strategy is to keep records of student performance and make them available to the student so that those aspects of the skill that need additional instruction and practice can be determined.

2. *From the student.* The student must be able to provide himself with appropriate feedback—that is, he should learn to monitor his own performance. In order to do so, the student should understand the principles underlying the skill—that is, not only how to perform the skill but know the reasons underlying the "how." The teacher can help the student acquire this capability by teaching the relevant principles to the student. You can also emphasize the reasons behind corrective feedback given to students by asking the student to analyze his own performance, by demonstrating good and poor performance, and by asking students to explain the differences and the underlying reasons. Another useful procedure for self-evaluation is for the student to keep a record of his performance so that he can note progress and areas needing further practice.

The initial stages of skill learning are characterized by the presence of many mediating responses (for example, thinking "C sharp" when you see the symbol on a sheet of music). If a student is to become proficient in a skill, most of the mediating responses need to be extinguished (when you see the symbol for C sharp, you immediately strike the appropriate key). The procedure which is used to accomplish this is practice: repetition of the skill until it becomes automatic. Your observations of students' practice will be a primary source for evaluation during instruction and will provide the basis for most of your feedback to students.

SKILLS: LESSON FOR ANALYSIS AND EVALUATION

LESSON	ANALYSIS
T: Today we'll learn the correct way to hit a wood shot off a tee. This is the most frequently hit shot during a round of golf. You'll hit a wood off a tee 14 or 15 times during 18 holes, and of course you want to hit the ball where it'll be in good position for your second shot. So don't try to kill the ball. A 250 yard drive out of bounds costs a lot more strokes than a 180 yard drive in the fairway.	Objective stated. Reasons given for importance of skill. These should enhance motivation if students are interested in golf in the first place.
Now, you've all done some driving before, so why don't you hit 5 or 6 balls now to warm up, and then we'll discuss the swing. (Students hit warm-up shots while teacher observes.)	Initial performances provide evidence for readiness—all students involved.
T: All right. Several of you have hit a shot or two very well, but most everybody is either topping or slicing the ball at least some of the time. And of course you want to hit the ball straight so you aren't always in the rough or woods. So let's review the grip and then work on that swing. Now your grip is very important—if it isn't right, then you don't have much chance of hitting the ball where you want to. Jeff, would you show us the correct grip.	Teacher seems to have observed carefully. Need for more reinforcement of effort? Component skill reviewed.
(Jeff demonstrates) Okay. Check your own grips and make sure that yours is like Jeff's. (Teacher moves to various students to check grips.)	Student demonstration. Will this be reinforcing for the student? The class? Good individualized attention.
Okay. Now no two persons' grips will be exactly the same, just as no two swings will be exactly alike. We're all built a little differently—shorter arms or different heights—and so everyone's swing will be a little different. But there are certain basic things about the swing that won't vary.	
There are three basic parts to a successful golf shot: the grip, the stance, and the swing. Now we've checked your grip, so let's consider the stance. First of all, your feet should be square to the line of flight of the ball. What that means is that if you draw a line connecting your toes and extend it, that line would be the same as the flight of your ball. Lay your club across the front of your feet like this (teacher demonstrates) and see if that is how your feet are lined up.	Component skills identified.

LESSON	ANALYSIS
(Students check stance.) Now, take some practice swings until you feel comfortable. Yes, Bob? S: How far apart should our feet be? T: About the width of your shoulders for a wood shot, although they can be a little closer if it feels more comfortable. (Students take practice swings while teacher moves around observing and commenting to individual students.) T: Now, let's work on the swing itself. There are three things that you need to practice now. First, start your backswing by bringing the club head back in a straight line from the ball like this (teacher demonstrates). Then, as you bring the club back, let your weight shift over to your right foot (teacher demonstrates). As you bring the club head up, keep your right elbow down close to your body and your left arm straight and close to your body (teacher demonstrates). Okay, I'll demonstrate some of these things, and I'll do some wrong and you tell me what I'm doing wrong. (Teacher demonstrates and students identify incorrect technique.) Now, practice the backswing until it feels comfortable. (Teacher observes and comments to individual students.) All right. Now let's take the rest of the swing. There are three things to remember. First, you begin your downswing with your hips, shifting your weight to your left side, like this (teacher demonstrates). Don't start down with your hands or you'll top or hook the ball. Next, keep your head down until you hit the ball. Don't worry about where the ball is going—you'll see it. The last thing is to follow through. Bring the club through the ball and up in an arc over your head. The best way to do this is to imagine throwing the club head straight after the ball and up. I'll swing in slow motion (teacher demonstrates).	Second component skill practiced. Additional component skills identified. Reasons are not given for these various steps. Should they be given now or later? Teacher uses observation and verbalization to reinforce and determine learning. Component skill practiced.

LESSON	ANALYSIS
Now, I'll do some things wrong and you tell me what's wrong with what I do and what I should do to correct it. (Teacher demonstrates and students identify incorrect behaviors.)	Again teacher uses observation and verbalization to reinforce and determine learning. An alternative would be to have students describe correct behavior.
Now, you can practice the whole swing in pairs, one swinging and the other observing. Help each other out when you see a problem. When you feel comfortable with the swing and ready, raise your hand and I'll check it out, and then you can practice your swing hitting some balls.	Integrated skill practice begun. Students used to help one another. Instruction individualized.
S: Can't we just hit some now?	
T: I know it's fun to hit them, but get your swing in shape first. Get in pairs now and work on the swing.	Desire to take some shots used to motivate performance of desired behaviors.

SKILLS: SUGGESTED ACTIVITIES

1. The check list below will be helpful in describing whether the teacher performed important teaching functions when teaching a skill. During or after the lesson, simply check off those which were attended to.

_____ The objective was stated.

_____ The expected level of performance was reasonable for my ability and the available time.

_____ The skill was demonstrated by teacher or through other means.

_____ Practice was provided.

_____ I understood the task well enough to monitor my own performance.

_____ The teacher gave me feedback.

2. Before teaching a skill in the lab, try out different instructional strategies on some friends. Specifically, try the whole and part strategies, and experiment with teaching the component behaviors in a forward order (starting with the first and working through to the terminal behavior), and in a reverse order (learning the final behavior and building up toward the initial behavior in the sequence). You might also vary your feedback—for example, early or late in instruction, or wait until the student seeks feedback, or ask the student to analyze his own performance. For what skills and under what conditions do these different procedures seem most effective.

3. We have all probably been embarrassed at one time or another when we have performed poorly at some skill. With a group of your colleagues, describe some of these occasions and the circumstances under which they occurred. What were the subsequent effects on your behavior? Did it motivate you to increased effort or result in your avoiding further attempts, or cause you to set more realistic goals? What could a teacher have done that would have averted the situation, or that would have helped you accept it more easily?

chapter 11

Learning Objectives

The preceding four laboratory lessons represent one way to conceptualize learning objectives, namely, that learning objectives consist of four types: concepts and principles, problem-solving, attitudes, and skills. While this approach is consistent with the way that objectives are often viewed by teachers, it is not the only way, nor necessarily the most appropriate for conceptualizing classroom learning.

Possibly this classification of objectives is too broad, subcategorization being necessary before you have identified meaningful objectives. For example, there are several kinds of attitudinal objectives, and certainly different strategies are more appropriate for achieving some of these objectives than for others. Furthermore, an objective that is of primary concern to you may encompass more than one of the learning types described in this manual. You may wish to combine two or more of the learning objectives and also to blend several teaching strategies in order to achieve a meaningful lesson. Finally, you may find that conceptualizing objectives in an entirely different way may have greater pay-off—that is, another system of classification may reflect more accurately the kinds of learning objectives which you consider important and provide a more useful basis for generating effective teaching strategies.

This chapter presents brief descriptions of several approaches to categorizing learning objectives. These descriptions are not intended to be complete nor to cover all possible types of categories. Rather, they are presented to give you some new ideas on how learning objectives can be conceptualized.

Your task is to develop a lesson without depending on the particular conception of learning presented in the preceding four chapters. You may draw from the approaches presented in this chapter, or you may generate an entirely different type of objective. In addition to developing an objective for your lesson, you will need to generate an appropriate teaching strategy. Then, as in past lab lessons, you will try out your teaching strategy for achieving your learning objectives.

The basic teaching tasks will continue to be relevant to analyzing your "unique" lesson. You should clarify objectives, determine those aspects of student readiness that are important for the acquisition of the objective, provide motivating conditions, and evaluate the outcomes of your instruction. In addition, you may wish to develop an observation form, whereby an observer can provide feedback to you about your teaching behavior and/or the effects of the lesson on your students.

SYSTEMS FOR CLASSIFYING LEARNING OBJECTIVES

Three general systems for classifying educational objectives are summarized in this section. You should consult the original references for more complete treatment.

Bloom-Krathwohl's Taxonomies

This system defines several kinds of "cognitive" and "affective" objectives. The cognitive objectives include six major categories differentiated in terms of their complexity. The affective objectives have been differentiated along a continuum of internalization, with five major categories.

A. Cognitive Objectives

1. *Knowledge.* This category includes recall of specifics, that is factual information. The specifics may range from particular names or dates to principles and theories. Appropriate application of different types of knowledge is not involved, only accurate recall.

2. *Comprehension.* Behavior that demonstrates understanding of some communication (written, verbal, graphic) is denoted by this category. To state the meaning of different parts of the communication or to restate the communication in other terms (translation), to reorganize the information or to draw inferences from it (interpretation), or to use the information in combination with other sources in arriving at a prediction (extrapolation) are all sub-classes of this category.

3. *Application.* This category denotes the use of knowledge in new situations. It includes the use of ideas, rules, or methods in the solution of problems. The unprompted use of knowledge is emphasized.

4. *Analysis.* These behaviors consist of the breaking down of a communication into distinguishable parts and showing the relationships between the parts. It emphasizes the conscious observance of specified logical processes.

5. *Synthesis.* Creating something is emphasized in this category. This includes both divergent thinking and creative application of knowledge to new problems, or to the generation of new problems. Synthesis objectives require the student to propose a unique solution to a problem or to create a product (a

painting, essay, floor plan, machine part, theory, etc.). The criteria for judging these solutions or products depend more on how the student defines the problem than on external criteria.

6. *Evaluation.* These behaviors include judgments about the value of some product, communication, event, or situation. Explicit use of criteria (either those generated by the student or defined by others) in making judgments is emphasized in this category.

B. Affective Objectives

1. *Receiving (or attending).* This category implies that the student is conscious of the occurrence of some particular class of stimuli, is willing to attend to these stimuli, or is able to focus his attention on what is relevant. This category is considered basic to affective behavior in that it must occur for any further development. Examples of behavior indicative of receiving are selection of relevant attributes or examples, preference for or choice of alternatives (but not necessarily based on adequate understanding), identification of appropriate examples or characteristics, and listening.

2. *Responding.* This category denotes behavior indicative of interest—that is, the student is doing more than merely attending. He is either complying, willingly responding, or experiencing some enjoyment through his response.

3. *Valuing.* Objectives incorporating this affective category imply that that associated behavior or its goal have value or worth to the student. He accepts the value (principle) as important or worth striving for; he chooses among alternatives on the basis of the value, or he is willing to make public his value—that is, to make a commitment.

4. *Organization.* In this category the student begins to organize his values—that is, he learns to order his values in terms of their importance in particular situations. Examples are developing preferences for types of literature on the basis of explicit values or preferences for certain types of content because of known satisfactions derived from them. What differentiates this type of affective content from responding is the knowledge of the basis for the preference and the conscious choice of one or another value as being more relevant in particular situations.

5. *Characterization by a value or value complex.* The student behaves according to a consistent set of organized values. This includes behaviors such as objectivity, receptiveness to new information and willingness to alter behavior on the basis of changing conditions.

Taba's Hierarchical Skills

This system delineates three levels of cognitive objectives: (1) concept formation; (2) generalization; and (3) application of principles. These categories are hierarchical so that before a student can properly apply particular principles, he must be able to generalize—that is, he must form the principles. And prior to this, the student must have developed the necessary concepts included in the principles. Appropriate instruction is thus seen as progressing gradually through these three cognitive skills. Each of these three cognitive skill levels is in turn subdivided, and learning and instruction are viewed as optimally progressing sequentially through each subtask.

A. Concept Formation: Level One

Concept formation includes three types of student behavior: (1) listing or stating observations regarding a stimulus object or situation, (2) grouping or combining similar observations or common characteristics and stating the basis for grouping, and (3) labeling or naming the common characteristics.

B. Generalizing: Level Two

At this level students can use previously learned concepts to describe differences and similarities among several situations. They can extrapolate beyond the immediate data to form generalizations. Within the cognitive skill of interpreting, the student progresses from identifying particular characteristics and concepts as being important, to relating these concepts, perhaps causally, and finally to generalizing the relationships to other situations. In order words, this level generally requires comparing several situations or problems, identifying concepts which distinguish (perhaps causally) the situations, and generalizing on the basis of their observations.

C. Application of Principles: Level Three

This category includes the following sequence of behaviors: (1) predicting a consequence and forming hypotheses to explain unfamiliar problems, (2) providing support and reasons for the prediction or hypothesized consequence, and (3) defining the limiting conditions under which the prediction or consequence would or would not be true. This last step requires logic and/or facts for support.

Hullfish and Smith's Reflective Thinking Skills

Reflective thinking or the process of supporting beliefs or assertions is conceptualized by Hullfish and Smith as consisting of three types of behavior: synthetic behavior, analytic behavior, and valuing. Each of these three functions can be viewed as distinct categories for learning objectives.

A. Synthetic Behavior

This category includes behaviors of fact finding—that is, forming and supporting beliefs or assertions which deal with the world of experience (phenomena in time and space). For example, the statement "Candidate X will receive at least 40 per cent of the vote," is a synthetic statement which can be supported or refuted by evidence (although note that synthetic statements are always probable in nature—never being absolutely true or false—subject to change in view of new evidence).

B. Analytic Behavior

These behaviors include the elaboration of the meanings and relationships of words and other symbols. Analytic tasks are definitional—the support of analytic statements depends not on facts from the world of experience, but rather from a rule book which defines a particular system (e.g., a dictionary or a book on symbolic logic). All statements include words which can be subjected to analysis as to their meanings. In addition, some statements are completely analytic in nature—that is, their support depends on reference to some system and not to evidence from the world. For example, "Two plus two equals four" and "All candidates for office are politicians" are definitional in nature.

C. Valuing

A third kind of behavior involves preferences—for example, "I believe candidate X *should* be elected to public office." Often such statements are impossible to subject to verification, being only a matter of personal, subjective preference. However, when such statements are made in terms of consequences—"'*If* candidate X is elected to public office *then* such and such will transpire"—then evidence becomes relevant. Also the words used in statements of value judgments are open to analysis.

Several alternative ways to conceive of different types of learning have been presented. At this juncture, you can select a particular type on which to base a lesson. Your choice may be influenced by a number of factors: the particular conception describes your content better than others, it suggests useful teaching procedures and activities, or it is a novel approach.

Whatever the type of objective you select, you will need to develop a teaching strategy to implement it. In doing so, you may use modifications of the strategies presented in earlier chapters, as well as strategies you invent or adapt from other sources.

LEARNING OBJECTIVES: SUGGESTED ACTIVITIES

1. You can provide for feedback procedures that will be relevant to your lesson and useful to you. In other words, along with developing your own learning objectives, you should probably structure to some extent the feedback you will subsequently receive about your lesson. Although this feedback will be unique to your lesson, we can suggest some general guidelines.

a. Develop criteria for your lesson that are most important to you. Then frame these criteria into questions that you can ask after you have taught the lesson or that you can give to observers to attend to during the lesson.

b. Because the criteria you select for feedback may not include aspects of your lesson that are most important to your students, you should provide for open-ended criteria. For example, a question such as, "If I were to teach the lesson again, what should I do differently? . . . or the same?" will allow for feedback that you may not have considered.

c. When possible, try to describe your strategy in behavioral terms—for example, you might list teaching behaviors which would facilitate or retard student attainment of your lesson objective, or list student behaviors that indicate progress toward the objective. An observer can then use this list to focus his observation and later to provide you feedback about your teaching and its effect on the students. A review of the observation procedures in chapter 2 and the observation instruments presented in the chapters on basic teaching tasks (3-6) should help you develop such a list.

2. References:

The systems presented in this chapter have been summarized from the following books:

Bloom, B. S. and others (eds.), *Taxonomy of Educational Objectives, Handbook I: Cognitive Domain.* New York: David McKay Co., Inc., 1956.

Krathwohl, D. R., B. S. Bloom and B. B. Masia, *Taxonomy of Educational Objectives, Handbook II: Affective Domain.* New York: David McKay Co., Inc., 1964.

Taba, H. and J. L. Hills, *Teacher Handbook for Contra Costa Social Studies, Grades 1-6,* 1965, which may be ordered from Rapid Printers Lithographers, Inc., 733 A St., Hayword, Calif.

Hullfish, H. G. and P. G. Smith, *Reflective Thinking: The Method of Education.* New York: Dodd, Mead & Co., 1964.

Appendix

CROSS REFERENCES WITH REPRESENTATIVE TEXTS IN

BASIC TEACHING TASKS

	DETERMINING READINESS	CLARIFYING OBJECTIVES	MOTIVATING
Alcorn, Kinder & Schunert	19-38	63-136	139-213, 313-75
Ausubel & Robinson	174-273	25-37	351-87, 445-49
Blount & Klausmeier	237-39	264-65, 278	81-88, 473-506
Clark	81-111	32-55, 145-68	112-41, 307-41
Clark & Starr	26-49, 161-202	97-158	50-94
Cronbach	88-267	30-67	466-538
DeCecco	54-127	30-73	128-81
Hoover	1-24, 234-323, 473-98	47-91	92-117, 122-233, 379-401, 447-71, 584-608, 632-59
Inlow	138-44	131-38	338-90
Klausmeier & Goodwin	94-136, 494-531	25-57	423-61
McDonald	463-95, 520-35, 642-79	80-88	109-159
Mouly	241-94	————	60-100, 332-59
Walton	155-63	144-55	261-305

Note: Page numbers indicate text material related to the laboratory task indicated by the column heading.

Alcorn, M. D., Kinder, J. S., and Schunert, J. R. *Better Teaching in Secondary Schools.* 3rd. ed. New York: Holt, Rinehart & Winston, Inc., 1970.

Ausubel, D. P. and Robinson, F. G. *School Learning: An Introduction to Educational Psychology.* New York: Holt, Rinehart, & Winston, Inc., 1969.

Blount, N. S. and Klausmeier, H. J. *Teaching in the Secondary School.* 3rd. ed. New York: Harper & Row, Publishers, 1968.

Clark, L. H. *Strategies and Tactics in Secondary School Teaching.* New York: The Macmillan Company, 1968.

Clark, L. H. and Starr, I. S. *Secondary School Teaching Methods.* 2nd ed. New York: The Macmillan Company, 1967.

Cronbach, L. J. *Educational Psychology.* New York: Harcourt, Brace & World, Inc., 1954.

EDUCATIONAL PSYCHOLOGY AND CURRICULUM AND INSTRUCTION

LEARNING TASKS

EVALUATING	CONCEPTS & PRINCIPLES	PROBLEM SOLVING	ATTITUDES	SKILLS
413-561	————	————	————	————
571-601	478-503	504-45	————	274-303
251	89-95	89-95	101-5	96-100
385-442	106-9			
342-85	169-244	169-244	————	————
349-442	————	————	————	————
539-72	394-406, 314-48	349-96	423-64, 616-58	270-313
607-99	385-427	428-79	————	273-384
529-80	25-44, 350-78	350-78	————	————
252-337	————	154-56	————	————
577-665	211-55	256-300	342-449	301-41
579-630	160-251	252-306	307-85	386-419
415-47	360-80	381-414	451-542	170-73, 310-20, 326-28
211-60	————	————	————	————

DeCecco, J. P. *The Psychology of Learning and Instruction: Educational Psychology.* Englewood Cliffs, New Jersey: Prentice-Hall, Inc., 1968.

Hoover, K. H. *Learning and Teaching in the Secondary School.* 2nd ed., Boston: Allyn and Bacon, Inc., 1968.

Inlow, G. M. *Maturity in High School Teaching.* Englewood Cliffs, New Jersey: Prentice-Hall, Inc., 1963.

Klausmeier, H. J. and Goodwin, W. *Learning and Human Abilities: Educational Psychology.* New York: Harper & Row, Publishers, 1961.

McDonald, F. J. *Educational Psychology.* Belmont, California: Wadsworth Publishing Company, Inc., 1965.

Mouly, G. T. *Psychology for Effective Teaching.* New York: Holt, Rinehart & Winston, Inc., 1968.

Walton, J. *Toward Better Teaching in the Secondary Schools.* Boston: Allyn & Bacon, Inc., 1966.

NOTES

NOTES

NOTES

NOTES